salmonpoetry

I0895895

BY THE SAME AUTHOR

POETRY:

Sailing Lake Mareotis (Salmon Poetry, 2011)
A Tour of Your Country (Salmon Poetry, 2008)
Refuge at DeSoto Bend (Salmon Poetry, 2004)
The Crosses (Salmon Poetry, 2000)
Iron Mountain Road (Salmon Poetry, 1997)
Dyckman-200th Street (Salmon Poetry, 1994)

PROSE:

Writing the Irish West: Ecologies and Traditions
(Univ. of Notre Dame Press, 2011)
From the Sin-é Café to the Black Hills: Notes on the New Irish
(Univ. of Wisconsin Press, 2000)

EDITED:

James Liddy. On American Literature and Diasporas
(Arlen House/Syracuse University Press, 2013)
James Liddy. On Irish Literature and Identities
(Arlen House/Syracuse University Press, 2013)

Junction City

New & Selected Poems 1990-2015

EAMONN WALL

salmonpoetry

Published in 2015 by
Salmon Poetry
Cliffs of Moher, County Clare, Ireland
Website: www.salmonpoetry.com
Email: info@salmonpoetry.com

ISBN 978-1-908836-87-8

COVER PHOTOGRAPH: St. Louis Arch, Missouri © Mwaits | Dreamstime.com
COVER DESIGN & TYPESETTING: *Siobhán Hutson*
Printed in Ireland by Sprint Print

Salmon Poetry gratefully acknowledges the support of
The Arts Council / An Chomhairle Ealaoín

the arts council an chomhairle ealaíon | funding literature | artscouncil.ie

Ten more miles, it is South Dakota.
Somehow, the roads there turn blue,
When no one walks down them.
One more night of walking, and I could have become
A horse, a blue horse, dancing...

JAMES WRIGHT
"Sitting in a Small Screenhouse on a Summer Morning"

Acknowledgments

New Poems have appeared or are forthcoming in the following journals: *Bunchgrass Anthology*; *Cyphers*; *Galway Review*; *The Irish Times*; *Scaldy Detail 2013*; *The SHOp*; *The Stony Thursday Book*; *Tampa Review*.

Special thanks are due to Villanova University for the award of the Charles W. Heimbold Chair in Irish Studies 2014, where this collection was assembled. I am grateful to Joseph Lennon, Nathalie F. Anderson, Daniel Tobin, Christine Casson, Pascale Guibert, Niall Wall and Paul O'Reilly of Scallta Media, Kevin Higgins, and Susan Miller DuMars for support. My families in the US and Ireland have provided great assistance over the years. And thanks, as always, to Drucilla Wall, Matthew Wall, Katie Woods, Caitlin and Jericho Jones.

I am also indebted to Dr. Joel Glassman, director of the Center for International Studies, and Dr. Richard Cook, chair of the English Dept., both at the University of Missouri-St. Louis, for facilitating a leave of absence to complete this project.

Contents

The Gathering Suite

(2015)

FOR THE GATHERING

I like it here / and I won't go back / where I came from.
LAWRENCE FERLINGHETTI *A Coney Island of the Mind*

Leaving Enniscorthy on the 555PM bus for Dublin
In the early evening darkness of January 13, 2011,
Christmas lights were strung from poles along the quays:
I could see from across the river a waiter in the Italian restaurant
Putting order to his stock of bottles at the bar, what I took for optics
Glistened behind him as ice crystals are wont to do on my home
Block in Missouri, on tops of banks of snow. As I was setting out,
There was everywhere dense liquidity—in the air, on walkers' faces,
And on the river's steamy surface, driven by snowmelt digging down,
Pummeled on by herds of oxen. My daughter and I were seated
Side-by-side. The driver stood on the footpath smoking.
Looking across the Slaney, I caught the waiter's starched shirt,
Cordials, aperitifs, spirits, liquids catching light, and a background
Row of wines: the reds muted, solid, all knowing. Traffic pressed
On the road sending dense rhythms deep into the earth, her pulse
Dropped for winter. I thought then that rather than depart I would like
To remain another day or two, dine again on Mick Wallace's pasta
And prosciutto, walk the narrow path to my childhood home
Come closing time. Though there's talk again of trawling up
One mighty gathering of émigrés, we know it is impossible to collar
Shoals rendered so long invisible. So, Ireland, I seek the quiet justice
Of my daughter's sleeve, absorb the fragrance of dark-brown hair:
We are members the proud diaspora rolling out-of-town. My father's
Face fully lighted-up and laughing I would never see again. The driver
Takes his seat. Roll on my river, roll. Roll on river, lead me home.

MISSOURI RIVER RUNNER BROKEN DOWN TRAIN

After Tomas Tranströmer

Descended by steps, Amtrak, stranded
Train, winter mid-Missouri, snowy
Fields, fallow, and the great stillness
We attribute to landscapes, named
By rusty pioneers who had earlier passed
These old signposts on horseback,
Westward ho wagon train. Some passengers

Remain onboard, others take to the air:
My companion is kicking her shoes, one
By one, against the lowest step. Lights
From the capital flicker a dull horizon into life.
Once, Mormons had assembled here.

Speak, all of my dead ancestors across
The ocean say, of America's rich core
For we imagine its twin lies somewhere on the line
Linking Tullamore and Clara. Is this a tidy
Supposition? Be quick, old émigré, soon
The engineer will have the Missouri River Runner
Rolling on. Time is short. Tea is getting cold.

MY HISTORY TEACHER CALLS OUT TO ME ACROSS THE DECADES

for Fergus D'Arcy

He'd whispered out since winter's halt:
you might take this route it's not too late.

This morning turnpike's so lightly quiet,
great swaths of maize-land lie drying out

as I drive over asphalt and concrete bridges
in search of New Harmony/Robert Owen as

on drafts above hawks hover like amphibian
sharks. It was in the concrete jungle, fog

hanging in the Dublin air, New Lanark
he mentioned and Ralahine: my history

lecturer was a learned man with jet-black
hair, I one scruffy ruffian, the duffle coat

in our age held de rigueur. From a Dublin
beauty two rows up—I still recall her

auburn hair—and native gods, he ever
so gently my gaze averted: O'Connell,

Cosgrave, and Michael Collins, crew-cut
heads in their native lair. He reclaimed

for history ordinary lives—our fathers
at threshing, our mothers at looms—

the world as I'd known he turned upside
down. Exit New Harmony is but two miles.

Dear Fergus D'Arcy, we are almost home.
New Harmony, Indiana. My teacher smiles.

OPOSSUMS: CITIZEN'S LAMENT

1.

Each spring opossums dawdle
out of hibernation to feast
on wild cherries, ripened
on a copse above their habitation.

Cherries fallen to the road induce
opossums: a trio gathered
this afternoon oblivious to the traffic
racing by on Brentwood Blvd., the urge
to eat strong as the need to procreate.

At a distance on a curbstone, I sit
and ruminate. Always, I admit
pride in being named American:
I count my blessings, offer prayer
for those put in harm's way to keep
us safe. Two small stars and stripes
displayed upright on the front porch
of our home will invite you to take
your ease—cup of joe or ice-cold
beer if you prefer, chance to pass
an hour of idle gossip and conversation.

Today, my grandchild occupies the curb
with me: she wears a red dress,
in places her hair is caught by blue
barrettes; across Brentwood Blvd.
a tanker truck refills the gas station's
great tanks, two Harley riders are idly
smoking to the side: they are Peckinpah
desperados of the Obama age. In his odd
rectangular van, Mr. Allen, the mailman,
makes a kind maneuver to avoid disturbing
opossums as they eat. He is a veteran

of Vietnam. Our hearts are opened
by this most welcome April sun: in wild
bunches, flowers cluster everywhere.

2.

Do we need another carwash in Webster
Groves? Our city fathers have decided
so: parents, teachers, elected officials
always know what is right for us. Saws,
machines, and hatted workmen have come
to clear the copse, layer of concrete laid
on top of brown Missouri ground, flashy
building measured up to code and named
for Westport, a municipality located some
suburban miles away. If you drive south
on Brentwood Blvd, you will note
that Sullins' Phillips 66 has had many years
installed a fine machine for washing cars,
in addition to providing gasoline,
sodas and some sundry items for dining
on-the-go, the new monster rising
across the street, competition a métier
of capitalism, only the fittest will arrive
home alive to dine at dinner time. I know
that you, my friend, are pondering
the opossums' predicament and the felled
copse's fate: piled earth, bushes and cherry
trees by men violated, and, then, by backhoe
pulverized. So much of nature thrives
so well in our Missouri home, drained
by our great rivers, the Mississippi
and Missouri, that you will join us
on the curbstone, my grandchild and myself,
in mourning for America, sweet land
of liberty where nature, left alone, fairest
best: the scene where Atalanta meets
with Brentwood now one of utter devastation.

3.

I am no third-rate David Attenborough
therefore my tidy narrative ends neither
on a cautious nor a dismal note, opossums
having crossed the road to take up residence
beneath scrub and starter oaks at the wilder
edges of our own garden having safely crossed
the Rubicon of Lafayette Avenue. Rotund
and slow, their movements are easily
traceable at night: we sit in a darkened
upstairs room the better to observe. Today,
I saw affixed to mailman Allen's truck
this legend: *Kill not the Moth nor Butterfly,*
For the Last Judgement draweth nigh. He
turned left slowly merging onto Lafayette.

COFFEE WITH MADAME OVESHKIN

Long limbs of winter trees shade-shift
at twilight—once orange, then gray
myriadly flung about, disconcerting,
crooked from the wind's peculiar way,
chipped into memory, old opacity
accounting for second lives lived-out
centered USA. Missouri. Our Midwest.

This scene is framed through the wood
and glass of Madame Oveshkin's
living room—should you peer inside
from the avenue to catch it: blazing fire,
lamplight. We are sampling Dierberg's
pastries with our coffees, side plates
indecorously balanced at our knees,
darkness lending balance to your view.

She speaks to me of private things,
hope stirring through the room, of love
and saving face, Kiev as a little girl,
of red leather gloves her mother wore
as they stepped one morning up into
a halted tram, the war, by then,
not yet broken out, the future, yet,
a long and level path, the gloves,
mother never tired of saying, soon to be
replaced and blue.

We are two immigrants
passing a winter's afternoon, her voice
—soft, accented, hung from home—
unzips my own enough to find a thread
of who I once had been. She pauses
and this is my invitation to speak. All
broken glass of twilight finally gathered
into darkness, winter, my wry narrative
of transatlantic flight held safe and warm
within her silver gaze, her soft *lebensraum*.

WHEN THE TRAIN BEGINS TO MOVE I DESIRE

Leaning forward I peer into old brown carriages:
the conductor would smoke at the row nearest
to the lavatory. Once, I read *The Hawkline Monster*
returning from Easter break. Habits differed then.

Then, the world was ahead of me though
what comprised it the darkness along the line disallowed.
My soles have cracked from walking, my face lifted
upward to the sun has gauged unpredictably.

There is a whiteness grafted to this train. Chilled,
I recline in near-empty carriage dross
of signage: separated sheets of newspapers, cups,
three Q Tips at my feet. Exterior still deep as winter life.

Now, the white train has begun to move. Nowadays
to smoke onboard is to risk a hefty fine, Gardai
stand in wait to apprehend at Wicklow or another
station further down the line. Havarti and olives,

I think, some cuts of bread. A glass of beer to wash
it down. I own a soft spot still for Richard Brautigan.

UNWINDING THE IMMIGRANT

Here on the prairie there is nothing to distract attention from the evening and the morning, nothing on the horizon to abbreviate or to delay.

MARILYNNE ROBINSON. *Gilead.*

You backward mark the daily planner on your bedside bureau. You think on rising, the winter sun warming the red-brick path, of mother standing before her hall-door rooting for her keys. You are concealed behind a delivery van; your American Dream—to hold her hand again. Iowa is silent, mostly.

You are lately returned from a homeland visit. You think: to sit for many hours among strangers in the bus depot in, let's say, Lahore or Limerick, is, for us, wound immigrants, a kind of salvation. If the 20:40 service to the capital is delayed another hour, we will have passed an extra day among the sycamores.

Your children move about your Iowa home as you, between places, count the icons on her kitchen walls and hold on a moment longer with the breeze at the roadside grotto, the yews healthy on the hills, the virgin having descended here once-upon-a-time.

There are no mountains on this prairie and scarcely, in most places, a copse of trees beyond huddled cottonwoods visible from the summits of the hills. Once, in Blair, Nebraska, you were witness to such a view, Seattle's Best and kitchen-table cries now thawing you awake.

Though considered flat, the prairie's gradient is as subtle as the floors of your century home, the child's golf ball guided by gravity from East to West to find its resting place against a hollow skirting board. Push against the crush of prevailing winds. And shuffle on.

On your Iowa returns, you uncoil—spools of tightened gut—upon the prairie. You wake after the first deep sleep, the plane trip undertaken, hard breath drawn at immigration, contented to have made land again, the gut run halfway already from its spool.

You phone mothers in, let's say, Lisbon or Louisburgh, to confirm that you are safely landed home. You eat a meal composed of what you have brought and from what has been bought from Hy Vee across the road. It is time to put the tea way, to whitewash over the buried life. Unseemly, surely, in American homes for immigrants to record the tear-wrought note.

Looking at the spool, you note how it has fully spun away, the gut-fine filament quite invisible to the naked eye. Unseen, your wounds will not distract sound colleagues from their urgent tasks. The natives of the prairie are rarely restless and this is the gift Iowans bring to their land.

You will not notice us, when you look out, when you walk across your prairie. We are the immigrant ghosts who wash your floors and, as doctors and nurses, utter kind words on hospice corridors when your loved ones have passed away. We are unwound from spools. The sun gone down, we are fallen into shadow.

Each night at home, you take an album to your lap, trace with your index finger the shape of your mother's face, and weep onto the prairie of opportunity, the washboard flatness each day passes though. There is neither distraction nor delay. Here in Iowa.

SONGLINES

By then ninety he flipped hands
so I might read the fable inscribed
on his soft washed palms. Self-
evident, old son, no bother now
with why or what or how: father
let me run my fingers along his lines.

Closing his eyes, my father breathed
with a lofty calm. I smelled onion
on his breath, chapstick richly coated
to his lips. Light of winter weak,
defined, found the curtain's slit, crossed
his crown as it wound across the room.

His lines I followed backward,
every strand ending neatly
tied with bows: green, red, white,
pink like roses and greens that grew
once in the garden he tended by the sea:
songlines of a father's life he yielded
up to me, two bodies joined together,
winter's afternoon, light and water
flowed. Traffic along a moving street:
he sought to pass his path along to me.

A GAME OF MARBLES

In part shadow of Dutch elms
boys gathered to roll marbles
formed a sacred trinity of circles;
our game's ring, drawn by stick,
was parted like a hot-cross bun,
round of players concealed
by an outer circle of onlookers,
each awaiting his turn to demonstrate
superior skills at marbles. Our
best players darted about the ring
like ghosts while weaker boys,
in some alarm, pondered
surrender of polished
chaney alleys. When it was not
my turn to play, I stood, happily,
for I was hanging with my homies
then, 1960s Ireland, transfixed
by urgent passion, boys playing
lobbers under Dutch elms
on John St. commonage, eyes
glaring up at me from the earth,
rain gathering twig and dust
to tentative pea soup. The dismal
school day, Tommy Brick
et aliqua had passed away,
my brown satchel, one among
many, discarded to the side.
Much of that school day
had passed in copying down—
lined pages, cursive hands—1916's
famed proclamation, over many
nights to be memorized, for it
was of some importance
to our nation, and even to our town:
of this, we had been reminded

by teachers, both clerical and lay,
words as mighty as flailing straps.
Outside the outer circle of onlookers
formed a broken corps of younger
boys. Their day would come.

WINDOWS ON THE WORLD

A winter's evening two strips of hair above his ears,
our parish priest making his duty call
describes dining this-time-last-week at Windows
on the World, just lately opened, as I take
the plate of Mikado from my younger sister, affecting
proper posture as I eat. His revival of the night
ignites my world, reverts our modest town to dimly-lit
and gray, uninviting shops, sourness drawn
outward from the pubs: the bookshop has shut-down,
no outlet's open to purchase *Motörhead.* I pledge
to get away. He recalls tasting lobster: he admired
the view of lights running up and down and all along
the Brooklyn Bridge. Next, the parish priest describes,
sinking deeply into my father's chair, and in rapt
detail, the 747's fuselage. To date, I have traveled
as far away as Dublin for the Spring Show
and borne witness at Leinster Finals—our yellow-
bellied warriors more catastrophic by the year—and,
the term lobster ringing from ear to ear, I have
yet to cross the Shannon I remind myself, being excused,
rising to leave the sitting room. Outside, this night
is cloudless and chill, I trace along Orion's Belt a path
to martini and profiterole, new terms I have this evening
plucked from holy air. I gawk through a narrow window
into the sitting room to observe our parish priest
drawing his palm across his face and I know by now
that my dear mother is desperate for a cigarette.
I count his many gold and metal fillings as he yawns
beyond the reach of his tardy hand: our parish priest,
Fr. John Murphy, ready to rise, has many calls to make
up and down our hilly, wet, oppressive, gloomy town.

WAITING FOR THE PADDLE STEAMER

My grandfather holds my hand in his
smoke issuing from his crooked pipe.

The paddle steamer's arrival fixed
for noon, all can board for half-a-crown

push upriver to the hills, disembark
at Baldwinstown. The sky is hard,

the river, I can recall, deep metal
gray, rebels gathered on Barkley Fell.

I watch a slim woman on the far quay
strip mannequins—first of colour, later

of their forms. The steamer has not come:
with serious formality, grandfather spits

into the Little Royal, releases my hand
to light his pipe. At home, mother speaks

disapprovingly of smoking, Look,
she cries, at Madame Fleur, crooked

roads converging about her eyes. I suppose
we will continue with our waiting

here. It will never come into view,
the paddle steamer. I know this. Our town

dies slowly as the days grow sultry
so I read, remove an apple from my bag.

My stepfather approaches mother's door.
Hark, the paddle steamer—near or here?

RETURNING TO INWOOD

In background you absorb resistant weight of traffic
Dispersing out across our bright American nation;
Another plane's about to occupy this space above
So it is but a single New York moment empty,
Cars and heavy semis headed-on for Riverdale.
The Henry Hudson is, you note, uncaring as a wave.

*

These abstract airy voltages hardly counted then.
Neither did you reckon backdrop of oldest oaks
nor the many chestnuts, maples and sycamores
So abundantly displayed in summer, though you did
Take daily pulse of the river, the Hudson pushing
Water eastward to mud flats, egrets fetched
And perched for all to see. You had been raised
In an old town, rains washing quickly to the sea.

*

Though on today's return you name and enumerate,
How ridiculous to seek all you had failed to observe
Two decades ago when, as a young immigrant
Wet in a strange land, you pushed a stroller uphill
In Inwood Park, pausing to pass a box of juice
To a walking child as he caught up. We held
Ground to converse with a gray-coated man
Who had survived the camps at Auschwitz.
He spoke of the Kennedys, his love of Germany
Startling, though later you had lived enough
To understand how bound are we to oak and bakery.
He had observed Michael Gold's *Jews Without*
Money among the diapers—his prompt to speak.

*

So intensely driven by the beat of newest lives,
Stroller-pushing on a path, curving down to water,
Lit by children's breath, angled to the East, you rarely
Caught dust of memory carried on the evening
Breeze. Dreamless, dead to the world, you slept nightly
Among the tired fathers, content on dry grassland.

*

Such are your thoughts today on this return.
It is late September; you sit in shade above the flats,
A gentle breeze blows across land and water.
With a final and indecent squeal, a train halts
At a nearby station on the river's other side.
And you hear the music of all of our children's voices
Carried across this city meadow on the willow wind.

from

Dyckman-200th Street

(1994)

THE GRASSY GARBAGE OF INWOOD

If anyone walks through here from out of town
he/she/it will hardly be pleased by grinding
boomboxes, the leaves of twenty autumns,
every brand of beer can, bottle, and cigarette
known to the bodega owners of this great city.
And I agree that Inwood Park is an unholy mess
and would be hard pressed indeed to write
the Fall/Spring/Summer/Winter verse *The New Yorker*
demands for each pristine season because I don't think
that he/she/it in the dentist's waiting room
in Cincinnati would like to read a nature poem
with a beer can in it. No way. Remember too
The New Yorker pays big money for nature poems.
Nevertheless, we are here as usual in the afternoon
and when we pass the first radio you wiggle your
little ankles to the beat and when I put you on the
grass you pull it as if it were the belly hair of paradise:
you find a *Winston* butt and show it to me before
diving into the vast anthropology of leaves. Your
mother said to me before we left the house: "Don't
let him near the trash," but what can I do,
a child must learn what his hands are for? Finally
it's time for the stream where a bird is drinking
beside a can of *Heineken Holland Beer*. You walk
on the stones, crouch, and let the water flow
through your soft fingers and I shout to *The New Yorker*
and the gardening weeklies that this is the natural world.
I take you away from it in tears, brilliant world
of grass and radios stretching out and bursting, and a
slinking butt lying there for you to notice it.

GREEN CARD

This day I head downstream
to surrender papers,

at the door I kiss you both
Son, Lover,

the flow of the Hudson
inevitable as every spoken word

as each threshed ear of corn
is there, and gone.

*

We are the paupers
on the road to Jerusalem
detraining at Chambers St.
on this early morning
of the light breeze a radio foretold:
wheat fallen on
stony opportunity.

TALL BLUE BUILDING/ FEDERAL PLAZA/TILTED ARC

Outside the tall blue building
a rusted metal structure
will soon be towed away because
federal employees do not like to look at it.
"An eyesore", they told the *New York Times*
and I don't want to judge a native piece of art
but I know some man laboured long and hard at it
and thought his work complete when it was taken away
from him. "Garbage", they shout well oiled in opinion
their boss "The Great Communicator,"
his father a drunk in Illinois and his son
has a bar called after him in Tipperary.
How will they take this structure away?
You can't strip metal limb from limb
apportioning moments spent by a river in another place
to section ten, line four, please print or type:
once I stared at your uncovered breasts,
often they dried me in huge towels to have me clean
for Sunday mass, or a rough hand rubbed my head
for some old thing I had once been able to do.
Turn the page and answer No to everything concerning
communism, culture groups, and political parties.
A woman without English pleads in Spanish
is turned from the screen by an officer of the State:
"Gawd, these dumb aliens," he whispers.
He is right. We know we are.
So what will they do with this rusted sculpture?
Will knives saw it up and clerks number it
in knackers' sections? I don't know but
when I came downtown to Federal Plaza it was this
eyesore which told me where I was.

AT THE EDGES OF THE NERVE: SONG FOR THE AMERICAS

At the edges sand and rocks lap the sea
body of a continent
relentless
but always this wondrous skin
of blue and gray

whatever I can imagine
is here

Rockaway Beach to
a roadway in California,
Alaska to Patagonia
to Darwin's bird lands

this skin of give and stone
holds it all
and freckled faces

and our griefs and possibilities
after all are nothing
there are no forms to fill

airplanes, sporting fields, trains,
these sturdy buildings where we live

in an instant I may walk another road
or watch the dust and sage brush grow

the skin of the human form
bathed in limes or mud,
but the blood flows

and morning comes in,

each day a door opens to street or field
edges survive their wind and water

and there is a belly of softness
beyond the apartment door to get used to,

I alight from the train in a new town
to change my clothes, and eat breakfast.

HART CRANE'S BRIDGE

Rows of immigrants facing west
behind, the Bridge
city onto itself, world
within world, poem
of boats, steel, sailors;
Amen to seagulls, shifting
riverbeds hold this nest
of cars. Submarines to
Brooklyn come up for air
Thomas Wolfe's dead, body electric
of America. To the right
a lady of the harbour
swathed in centennial
Band Aid. The paper says
the French repairmen will not
go home when the work's done.
What does Whitman mean?
What have our bodies built for,
definitions through paper or
sunsets in familiar places?
Where in the forest grows
the Green Card?
Is it what surrounds the primrose
on the Wexford road?
Sit under a pine
with food and open lips,
hold this child of ours
upwards to the sky
to bronze his skin
any sky, any where
only the Irish pines and primroses
are mine.
America,
how she deals the cards.

IMMIGRANTS

Family pictures crowd our walls,
we are haunted by the girls
we didn't kiss, by the jobs made for us
we didn't get. Lonelier than
the parents we left behind, the dull life
of the old country would be fast enough.
Our national colours are the flags
which aren't flown on Labour Day.

At night we go home to break our bread.
Our doors are bolted to America.
Our dreams fastened to no promised land.

SONG AT LAKE MICHIGAN

I walked to Lake Michigan
with thoughts of a sea nearer home
where we swam under clouds of departure
Suzie, my father, and me.

I walked towards Wisconsin's waters
to take wind of some boats and the rocks
a child of the green on the waterfront
faces of the past in my eyes.

This country is righting itself
working by day for the right not to sleep
galloping along without comment or thought
content that some time is at hand.

But here I can sing to myself
unbound by traditions of death
I'm not working for brothers or nuns
I'm drinking slowly at the wild neon bar.

RIVER SLANEY: NEW YEARS'S DAY

The purple flowers push into the air;
I stand between wall and water on New Year's Day.
The River Slaney moves downstream but returns
to fall as rain on Enniscorthy street and smoke.
Home again. Walking on the prom into the heaviness
of short pantsed hurling, hand in hand memory, and confusion
in summer about when and how the day might end. I do not
doubt the river now nor the insistent voices in the elms
excluding no one, but I have entered into other loves beyond
this solid town and landscape. A boychild builds
a snowman in a Pennsylvania backyard, a girlchild nurses
on her mother's lap and my lover, as she drinks her morning
coffee and feeds the future which will replace us, reads the book
I left in her Christmas stocking. But you sleep one night
in your parents' house and you have never been away; each
return and each departure are small discordances such as the fog
will be on the river as you leave New Ross on your way home
from a night's music. The doorbell interrupts the music but is
toneless to replace it. This purple day I relish my river
divided town, my voices on the phone, my well shook hand.

THE COUNTRY DOCTOR

He is standing at his door talking with the world as it crawls up Main Street to church, dogtrack, hurling game, and he tells me to stop smoking, that Redmond was a greater Irishman than Pearse.

We sat in his waiting room and they sat up late in cottages on the side of the mountain waiting for his car: the ascending car lights throwing odd shapes on cups, plates, and walls, jars of jam, cornflake boxes, and honey.

Dr. Bowe rode out into the night's romance to heal the sick to talk and talk and talk, beating his knuckles on your chest and bringing you back to life. You learned the history of County Wexford with the glass jammed under your tongue.

Hurling players walked down from Bellefield with cloths on their wounds. They lay on the doctor's couch while he threaded the gut slowly through, a fraction above the eye, as the soft voice droned on about the Black and Tans marching through Kiltealy. My brother as a child went to Dr. Bowe with the five pound fee, was given back a pound, told to keep it for himself, and to say nothing to our mother.

Like Samuel Beckett, another great Irishman, he slept by day and worked by night. He visited our houses when the work was done and made the family part of all examinations, gathered round the sick like Rembrandt's students, in The Hollow or out in Bree, all leaning over the doctor's shoulders as he explained.

His skeleton in the final embraces of air danced round the ballroom floor at my brother's wedding. I watched the parade come to shake his hand. He burned like Paul Klee's fire as we waltzed around him, all odd-shaped heads and organs. A one man welfare state, who valued talk more than he did the time. A Jesus come to heal us and teach us how to live. In the ballroom that last night. This morning walking up Main St. to the cathedral looking for your face.

from

Iron Mountain Road

(1997)

FATHER, FATHER

Having crawled through
the tiled catacombs under
the Port Authority. Heard

balls clattering behind
glass, check-it-out merchants

but Isaac Bashevis Singer dead
was the word on the street.

Stalled buses. Traffic lights
stuck on yellow, brownies
hugging meters, the Newsday
sign shattered on the sidewalk,
the national debt headstone
flickering, a mocking pulse,
Girls, Girls, Girls, The
Croissant Shop, The
New York Public Library
Bryant Park, sauerkraut and smoke
from vendors' carts.

You liked buildings with
courtyards like mine

and hearing your dead language
spoken in diners on Columbus Avenue.

The immigrant has witnessed two worlds
this much is true, the immigrant writer

is the witness' memory who pens lines
full of shame, lines full of hope.

Our leader has fallen. Our leader is dead.

MAGIC BARRELL MAN

for Morris Dickstein

> *If you walked away from a place they tore it down.*
>
> BERNARD MALAMUD, *The Tenants*

A daughter carrying books emerges from the subway into the smoky evening. Blue lights over the liquor store, men and cigarettes. A bouncing ball, Jackie Robinson.

The first seven years in the New World. Brooklyn, New York.

Two men sit in an apartment, the younger passing his elder words to give substance to the death of the family, Manhattan humming beyond the window panes.

The magic barrel man is my father, I'll have you know.

Cobblers, rabbis, and matchmakers waiting and weeping while the bride is stripped bare. To taste heat in one's mouth is to linger less painfully on these crowded avenues. It is not possible to be unhappy in America.

In Inwood, an old tailor has a heart attack on the side-walk while a broad-shouldered youth runs off with takings from his shop. And I am across the street watching the fracas like a man reading a book, or a foreigner watching a movie depicting crime in America.

I listen to the old tailor while my kids watch him draw licorice from the money drawer, and when they settle in to hear him make the Singer hum, I imagine him and me huddled in the corner of the shop seeking each other's warmth: father & son, teacher & student. Immigrants sitting in luminous silence: wealthy & wise & weeping.

But I hear the tailor's children have come and led him to the suburbs, just as he had led his brothers and sisters out of Germany, raising them as father & mother in America.

Soon the travel agency offering package tours to the Sandals resort in Jamaica will absorb his shop. Nothing remains but words. For you, proud fathers, these gentle signs are today added to the record.

THE WESTWARD JOURNEY

Setting out on the westward journey
with eight suitcases and two cats.
On this last night we sleep at the
La Guardia Marriott to swim in its pool,
begin the busy work of forgetting
Mr. Pedro's large hands stuck
in the till, his fingers floating amidst
the pennies. "You are leaving New York
to live in America," he says. "I would
be afraid of that, and the little ones
will lose their Spanish." At the end
of our street each Sunday morning bright
speedboats race for the early shadows
under the George Washington Bridge.
Immigrants: we depart from Inwood.

I have stored away your cries
of being born: these ugly streets,
red paint on the old benches in
Payson Playground, and those sweet
brown eyes of an immigrant from
Galicia fumbling and cursing quietly
about for our change. My own
childhood unimaginable without
the River Slaney humming "Son, you
breathe" as I read the clock each
morning above Louis Kerr's shop.
Impossible that there was another life.

Tonight, my children are singing in the
water at the prospect of a plane ride to
another life, but someone must remember,
there must be someone to write this down.

FOUR STERN FACES/SOUTH DAKOTA

I was living in a bedsit in Donnybrook
when John Lennon was shot outside the
Dakota apartment building in New York
and that's what I'm thinking this morning
piloting my family through the hollow
darkness on Iron Mountain Road, trespassing
on the holy ground of the Lakota nation.

Four stern faces in the distance address
me and when I get stuck after rattling off
Washington & Lincoln I call on my son to
fill-in the blanks and wonder how the hell
will I pass the civics test when I apply
for citizenship. I could tell you all
about Allen Ginsberg & Adrienne Rich
but presidents, state capitols and amendments
to the constitution would snooker me,
and I get the feeling the I.N.S. doesn't care
too much for postmodern American poetry.
My daughter belongs to the woods—mosses,
pine needles, slow moving light and shade,
a bright face in the back of the car
breathing a fantastic language, this
slow mid-morning pilgrimage I drive
my loved ones forward and climbing.

When Lennon was dying I was typing
the forms to come to America: on this
journey through the Sandhills—Irish sand
dunes without the sea—to the Black Hills
to wild flowers with names so gorgeous
I cannot bear to hear you say them.
Native people, "Strawberry Fields Forever,"
Ryan White dying in Indiana. My children
craving this just as the matchsticks and cats'

eyes on the Gorey road mesmerized them,
howling now for lunch. Here the light is
different, the evenings shorter, Gods are weeping.

And there's no escape from caring
or from history: to lie on high plains
prairie grasses, and Black Hills is to be
blown into their stories, drowned in
their summer rains. Just when I think I've
lost the Irish rings around the tree, I open
the door and find red clay stuck on the
tyres, the whole earth screaming, my children
breathing on the electric hairs above my collar.

Being woken one ordinary workday to Lennon
being dead, "Imagine" on the radio, remembering
the grown-ups weeping in late November '63,
one morning in Dublin when it finally struck
that heroes are flowers constantly dying on
these black and holy hills we spend the years
wandering towards till light reveals a universe
beyond stony victorious faces bolted to a rock.

FREEWHEELING BY THE PLATTE RIVER: A SONG

When I woke this Wednesday your hair
was spread on the pillow like the
many channels of the Platte River.

As I drive westward with trucks
into the absence of trees, corn, cuts
in the horizon, I fix on the browned
grass flecked with the end of snow,
on those signs of our ageing into
the life of the prairie in winter--
this cloister of Diet Coke, draws,
artificial creamer for your coffee,
and too much country 'n western on
the radio. At night you roll against
me for my warmth. I trace from the
backs of your knees to your highest
vertebrae the cities of this state
from Omaha all the way to Chadron.
You turn towards me trusting in these
warming motions naming grasses
awakening the soil to the secrets
you have come to plant. The Land
The Land you sing straw hat on
your knees and yes I have heard it
talk to you and the Platte River
calls your name to me this afternoon
and I imagine you shin-deep and skirts
raised dancing on a shallow bar
in the middle of the flowing.

When I woke this Wednesday your hair
was spread on the pillow like the
many channels of the Platte River.

FARM AID

The colours do not merge according
to the sun. The quilt is stable. As I
was taught the shapes of shells
and stones on beaches my hands explain
textures of soils and grasses, and
hear what torments the winds carry
from dying farms, truckloads of
families on the final trips to town.
This evening potatoes boiling,
salad made, the roast cooling I hear
Fr. Jones saying prayers for the corn,
and oats and barley in Star of the
Sea church in Riverchapel, County
Wexford. Returned from our drive
we listen to the Farm Aid concert
on the radio, children with crayons
at my feet dividing vast sheets of paper
into enormous Nebraska fields
of soy beans and corn. Immortal farm
families, enormous tombs on each
horizon, a wailing absence of young voices.

JUNK FOOD

The pumpkins are piled in a trailer
outside the 74 St. Albertson's, my
kids waiting in the car for happy meals
to appear through Window 2 of Burger
King—the fading October light, blowing
leaves, the ugliness of Dodge St. west
of 72nd makes me want to cry & the
song on the radio is so good it makes
me want to cry, but the children are
so happy with their disgorged bags &
Cokes it makes me want to say a prayer
& drive around again to order a bunch
of whoppers & my son reminds me
of the first time I drove up to a fast-food
joint when I was 37 seven years of age—
I didn't know you had to order at the
metal hole in the wall & drove
straight up to the window & told
the greasy kid what I wanted & he
couldn't believe I didn't know the etiquette
of ordering & that was the Mickey Dees
on Dodge so now I stick to the Home
of the Whopper across the street.

I know I'm
Slow—I was 28 before I learned how to
ride a bicycle & that was due to the fact
that (as the NYPD says) I was on the Aran
Islands where there is no public transport-
ation system. You have to turn the radio
down to hear yourself when you order
junk food & the greasy parrot always
shouts it back to you & when you have
an accent it takes a few tries to
get it right. But you see the children's

faces in the back of the car & you drive on
envious and freed because it's fiendishly
hard to find pleasure in the simple things
nowadays.

Soon
we'll be buying pumpkins, cutting
horrible faces, burning candles
& Dundee neighborhood will be full
of magical stories, milk &
pumpkin pie & the snows will
follow & my children will sled & I
will shovel & whistle &
parallel play before cooking
some dinner—but it won't be junk
food because I can't cook that good.

VICTORIA, BRITISH COLUMBIA

Green, dogwood trees, gnarled oaks
driftwood at Oak Bay. I am far
north in winter again where daylight
swifly evaporates, where morning is
as sodden as the parliament grass.
I have come to an outpost of empire
to encounter familiar separations
& eat familiar dishes. I remember
your long fingers like sticks in the
stones, your children asleep, my first
view of the Pacific in Mexico when we
lay exhausted & full of songs:
how this ocean makes me want to weep.
I think of the hard air of the prairie
which lurks in each winter maple &
the brilliant light of early morning.
I am soft-skinned, broken-kneed
oar-buried, man-of-war, Irish.

GREAT SAND DUNES/COLORADO

We drive
on the flat roads
of a high plateau

in the Rocky Mountains
to the huge dunes.

Twelve children
on their knees

bright hats like
sails on the water.

Smelling the sea
I fall among them

scooping water
to my face easing

my jeans into heavy
sand where once

the bottom-feeding
flounder ruled supreme

here in the Rockies
at the seaside.

KEARNEY & PLATTE & CRANES

I'll motor west to seek the crane voice river with the lovely name
and your poets, Nebraska,

who spoke among the coloured walls of Kearney & Zeami
your performances loaded as the large, empty corn fields
in the car beside me. You know it all: I have come to learn
this river and this land.

Over the wave paths of this ancient sea with the light
of the setting sun in the waves

clouds like banners which obey the ancient rules
of the state patrol keeping the world at 65 rocking the voids
of the westward sky.

When the moon rises the distant mountains are framed
& numbers emerge clearer & bluer from the dashboard.
Great waters toss and toss, the grey waves soak the sky,

for ten million years they have been coming to the Platte,
the Sandhill cranes.

ROOFTOPS & ILLUSIONS

> *Towns are the illusion that things hang together somehow,*
> *my pear, your winter.*
>
> ANNE CARSON, *Plainwater*

I sweep a flat space among the many-levelled sloping roofs of this grey town. Slate and felt. Cars parked from St. Aidan's down Main St. I hear on the wire that Jesus will save us, that the cathedral restorations are simply gorgeous.

In her studio on the Market Sq. Mrs. Carty fills in the edges of a photo the camera lost from scratchings in her lap—communion girls. Blue skies, deep-red missals, puffs of cloud.

Wildflowers are growing out of the walls, the gutters are weighted with moss. White dots on the grey crown of the Athenaeum, the domino roofs of Slaney St. I touch your knees & smell your breath as blood flows from your orifices into the Slaney. You whisper dissolution, departed children.

At seventeen I lay in bed hearing prayers under bunting & bridges for the Sacred Heart. I was thinking about the walkers stuck on the hills in white dresses/sashes, waiting for the marching to resume so I might continue with the rhythm of my reading.

To know I suppose one day I have longed forever to describe to you. Childhood was a day when only the surfaces counted, when we found the goalposts in murky water near the Mill Field and made plans for retrieving them.

When we stripped in the heavy night air under wild fuchsia and stars and watched cars come and go on the Wexford Road. We are easily replaced and forgotten, so skies and rivers are what we have learned to call discourse. I am one man—you need to know this—grey rooftop & water, undissolved by absence, crossing the old bridge from the Shannon to the other side of town.

from

The Crosses

(2000)

BLUES FOR RORY

From the Slaney Co. Wexford Mississippi Delta
rode the rails in flannel shirts, warm CIE beer
in hands, in the smoking carriage by big muddy cities
Gorey/Chicago, Arklow/St. Louis, moving on mile
by mile marker by great rivers getting closer still
to hearing the legendary bluesman from Cork City
play on his battered strat the blues, and sing I could've
had religion but my little girl wouldn't let me pray,
that kind of girl hard to come by in the Slaney
Co. Wexford Mississippi Delta though neither did
we pray too much being all prayed out since
Confirmation. Rory Gallagher at the National
Stadium after Christmas, the first live gig ever
for me except for wedding bands in the Slaney Co.
Wexford Nashville Tennessee as I served across
the counter large Macs to speeded up Country
Roads, couples gliding across the maple floor. All
confused in Connolly/Union Station the route to
Harold's Cross to breathe the raw elixir of the
blues, Rory Gallagher's sweat falling on his guitar.
I could touch his feet if the bouncers turned their
heads, who can describe the thrill of knowing it all
for the first time, first bottleneck solo couple of
numbers in? Lord, take that sinner boy home &
I'm here on the prairie now with new CDS
from Amazon.com, window breeze from the deep
south wafting from tree-lined street to tawny alley,
potholes open wide, the rusted trucks, loose gravel,
night light yellow flickering, where for hours
the repo man stood with his forms and magazines,
the world not so bright now for your absence,
Rory Gallagher, Can't believe it's true, I can't
believe it's true. How we walked by the Grand
Canal in wet midnight winter air, lost looking for
Ranelagh, electrified & silenced by the wonder
of it all, not caring if we ever made it home to
Model County Wexford, hotbed of hurling, home
of strawberries, fields of barley & country music.

THE CROSSES

We were driving back to Denver
from Don Martinez's funeral on an April day
under the clearest of skies,
the brightest of light.

Nights he read *On the Road* under lamplight
maps flattened under cold stars on lands
which could never know compromise,
whose quiet men towed his truck
to gas stations full of dust. They could never register
Don Martinez 's cadence, the soft lines of his face.

We sat together three of us on worn recliners,
drinking red wine on the porch,
under the western sky & above the boom-and-
bust Denver you despised. You watched
distant planes, flying low, lit for landing.
Your heroes: Janis Joplin, Joe Di Maggio.
Your worn face, impassive as cedar.

You underlined for me the desolation
of these highways: the mockery of
place names among great continuities:
rising to dryland, descending onto grass.
I was anxious to count the mugs on the
blue counter beside the sink, Marie's foot
hard on the pedal, passing faded shadings
of the Wild West, *Wilco* on the radio.

For Marie you came to Denver. From our bed
I heard your breaths from under jazz on the
radio station, as mellow late-night as your bodies,
as snow falling on parked cars on Decatur St.
Lightly touching my hands, Marie returned at
daylight, around us the blankets settling peacefully.

Under the crosses, you have joined the dry
ground. You passed time over reds & coffee
with waitresses as you crossed this earth
from Cody to Las Cruces slowed down by
quiet humiliations of migrant life: gas station oil
changes in Pueblo, arrest in Walsenburg for
disorderly conduct, trumped up charge &
hefty fine. Desperate in East Texas, you beat time
with your sister on slot machines, her husband
working an *Amoco* rig on the Gulf of Mexico.

We were driving back to Denver
From Don Martinez's funeral on an April day
under the clearest of skies,
the brightest of light. Under the crosses
he was joined the dry ground.

TOUR DE FRANCE/ENNISCORTHY

The greenery hung with rain
as the train approached our town

white blossoms on blackberry bushes
lowered their eyes, observing blood
on the trackside, blood on the rails.

Near first light one bright June morning
around the longest day, a Solsborough
cook, from an upstairs window, the
failing fires espied. General Lake all
attired to rout the rebel horde: the
mayhem of midsummer on Vinegar Hill.

Parked cars encircle the town. It's a battle
to buy a bag of Tayto and a pint of beer.
From American Fare aromas of vinegar,
burgers, & chips. A child will kill for a 99.

A sloping field so light of barley, breeze
pushing in from the sea: Turret Rocks,
new houses, the Wexford Road.

Who is dead? Who has fled?
Who lies in the ditches bleeding?

The greenery is dried of morning rain:
in other lives, we were croppies;
in other lives, we were yeos. I hear the
cries from Scullabogue & Fr. Murphy
quartered for four provinces in Tullow,
Co. Carlow. Chris Boardman descending
from the Duffry Gate: the tour is on its
way, two centuries counted in a single day.

The river moves lazily from distant hills to
distant shore, a comoradh day we alighted
lightly from the train, from a sudden cloudburst
into sunlight yellow as our Wexford fields.

Under the banners, under the flags
the peleton cyclists rode.
From pavement side & window ledge
we all clapped our hands and cheered.

THE ROAD

To begin again
after
travelling

the white car
outside
the motel

to have to
again
have faith enough

to pull
one door firmly
then walk away.

JUNCTION CITY

Expelled soft breath
collides with an early morning patch
of breeze come through a window
latched open to rusted barleycorn

so what is breathed out
joins the wind, a slice of yesterday
when sent to fetch a grown-up's cardigan
a child notices flash of light
in the modest wake of jet-ski
cutting across parallel to shore
Irish Sea.

On the road you take an old blue bus
suddenly hangs infirmly right
Junction City, E. Flint Hills Blvd.

so that outside La Isla del Encanto
you breathe euphoria of Kansas,
find oaks whose signs are known

to you and bales of hay covered in black
plastic and kisses as the road you travel
and the road you dream merge like

numbers on the Interstate. We share
one route home to fresh meringue
inhaled on a city street an ocean away

from the bakery through which I'd wandered
as a child, crossing a threshold

at the intersection. Don't you know your place?
My home is where I am, old wise blue bus.

PUYE, NEW MEXICO

Mesas, arroyos, evergreens call you back

a smooth ladder awaits your hands
to grasp wood for your climb
to the first level where you'll find again
medicinal, wand-like creosote. Noontime
water bottle slung over your blue shoulder.

The walls of Puye are dug out for food,
for love under the slanted stars in the chill of
evening.

But you have moved, as before,
toward the summit of clay
apartments. How small you are crouched
among the corridors.

How out-of-place you are
in the dark gathering place in the earth
to which you have descended to await

storytellers at this very moment wandering on
mountain streets from across the hills.

Mesas, arroyos, evergreens call you back
to the cool centre of the baked lands, mother
of roots, mother of the dew.

You have
wrapped the rope about your wrists, your
timber bones, your parched heart & dusted
shirt, miles away from your parked car.

CAHORE

Standing as we were, there was no getting beyond the surfaces
of Cahore

in mid-pier against the railing, a small boat chugging
angular towards

the slipway at the setting out of the Irish autumn, at
full tide

on an August evening, as towards the Blackstairs our muffled day
fell away.

We had driven out from Enniscorthy and wondered as we sat
what hours

lay ahead for us, as heavy, still, winter barley was dragged from
shorn field

to frantic town. Our children fish for crabs, hand lines hooked
with bacon

as youths leap from the pier's end, as across the cove the final waves
cover the

stony beach, smooth & salty, cool as aluminium, this intense
brightness before

the tide turns and the light fades, how cool it is to be alive
I think

heart on my sleeve, freed crabs running busily down the slipway
for seawater.

THE WESTERN MOTEL/EDWARD HOPPER

On a leg below her hemline
sunlight falls, her right knee raised
to the level of a parked automobile
as shadows creep nearer the fallen
dust of an empty service road.

Suitcases packed,
she's turned away from the charming,
the severe Colorado light.

As a young woman she pulled the covers back
& read in her swimsuit,
a French hotel room flooded with sunlight.

Another day, at eleven on the dot
naked in a blue armchair she looked
happily down at vendors on the street.

And later on, she'll be reading in a hotel
by the railroad. Her husband grey &
smoking, counting freight cars going by.

Hard always to find the moment to speak of love:
he is reading from sheets of paper,
she has placed an index finger on the ivory keys.

A bartender has filled the ice-buckets, wiped
down the counters & table tops at the
western motel: one vodka & lime, one gin & tonic.

WEATHER REPORTS

I watch children draw sleds from
garages behind their homes. Once I saw

a snowman on the Market Sq. Once the
Island Rd. was flooded to the upstairs

of the houses and canoes paddled
in dreams on the street, heads of petrol

pumps like buoys indicating the Slaney's
rise, the island disappeared & crowds at

the bottom of Slaney St. waiting for the
old bridge to go. My mother spoke of

1946 when the river had frozen.
Today, the sky spreads out to the Iowa

bluffs, snow on the ground, low clouds
dipped and winds wild Atlantic bound.

THE BAKEHOUSE

As Seán Lemass planned the
great leap forward, I walked
a concrete path between high-
limed walls on the dark
passageway to the bakehouse

by sheds full of coke and anthracite
bottles of methylated spirits hidden
under blocks in the corner kept
company by old rags
and a box of matches.

Looking up, I saw where
stone met cloud as I moved
through chill, familiar blindness
into the flour-white blaze where
trays of sponge cooled side-by-side
on metal tables by a window opened
wide to Jimmy Dale's yard where
weeds stretched hard under damp winter light.

The women talked about dances:
Brendan Bowyer & the Royal Showband,
Larry Cunningham & the Mighty Avons,
The Castle, the Barrowland Ballroom,
Adamstown, the home of country music,
"The Hucklebuck," the nation's favourite song.

On my corner stool, I watched them
fill sand castles with fresh cream, attach
wings to butterflies, decorate wedding
cakes with blue and silver balls, learned
what we mean when we say
"lustre" and "dough." I drank my tea and
wondered what would appear from the oven,
four score Christmas puddings hanging overhead.

DAY'S END

It's the lamp in the kitchen,
the greens from the garden
in the curved orange glass,

the tin of *Butter Nut* coffee
on your scratched blue barrette
box on late October evenings

I remember looking back, my
two hands placed on the faded
table cover, clock ticking along.

NEBRASKA/CHRISTMAS EVE

Greetings. The Platte River crawls across yellow prairie under concrete bridges to meet the brown Missouri. Rolling darkly down from kingdoms we know as South Dakota, Montana.

Greeted by neon towns where children are held in sleep by crimson horizons at the end of the world, where parents as they curl confirm majestic interiors of sorghum and corn, at the end of the day.

Greetings. Rivers on great journeys, our plates of food and sleep. We break bread under great skies. Our red faces know so deeply our mothers' feet walking on landings, like passing water over stone. A summer evening when we sat on rocks to await the passing of the evening train.

Greetings for this season. It is snowing heavily under a quarter moon so shingle and land groan, contentedly. Under the tree, presents are wrapped in red. The bows are white. As time rolls with the tree limbs, we arrive at the continent's door.

We have greeted the stranger. He sits hands wrapped around coffee cup before our open fire. The woman of this house and her children are sleeping. The man has cleaned the kitchen surfaces of crumbs and has confronted the clever spaces of the dishwasher, with his cups and glasses.

Hard to tell at this late hour the heart's direction, Nebraska. A summer evening when we sat on rocks to await the passing of the evening train. The river moving because it can't be still, the man greeting a white towel with his mother's hands.

from

Refuge at DeSoto Bend

(2004)

THE WEXFORD CONTAINER TRAGEDY 2001

Cormorants

From the huddle of their raucous queue,
schoolchildren seek names for the sleek,
dark seabirds they follow as they shove.

Cormorants, I say, then turn away. For
a girl who's removed her headphones,
then glares at me: CORMORANTS, I

say again. In Wicklow, I'd observed
them grouped on rocks beneath gannets,
the train trundling closer to the capital.

I wait to board a ferry for Ellis Island:
once a tower of hope and humiliation.
now a museum and shrine to immigration.

Reader

Gather close, dear reader, my tidy narrative goes like this.

Eight stowaways in the hold of the Dutch Navigator died. Lack of oxygen the cause.

On the Feast of the Immaculate Conception. The biggest shopping day of the year.

They were five men and three children who had paid to stow some harmless hours from Zeebrugge to Dover.

Like misfiled papers, they were loaded in error with new Italian furniture for Wexford Business Park. Sailed for two days on an unkind sea to dock at Belview Port, Co. Waterford, near to where in Norman times, Strongbow had married Aoife. A painting of this event dominates our National Gallery on Merrion Sq.

In time, these fierce Normans became Irish giving Wexford our castle at Ferrycarrig, as, long before, ferocious Vikings had given us our name.

In Wexford, the refugees meet the trained gloves of Dr. Harbison, Chief State Pathologist. Driven from port to business park, enjoying a Model County funeral prior to an accounting of their arrival. One hundred hours contained in all. England's whitest Dover their intended destination.

Great hatred, little room, out of Algeria, Albania, and Turkey they had come. Had they ever heard of Wexford, where for centuries we have watched hardy commoners and hale kings disembark?

"They met what I can only describe as a horrific death," the Irish Justice Minister explained. They had encountered smugglers and thieves in the biting corner of a dangerous town.

At the New York Holocaust Museum

Once, our family visited the New York
Holocaust Museum in Battery Park.
There is a moral to the exhibit beyond
what history teaches of love & hate,
study & action, kindness & betrayal.
It is this: get out while you can. Hard,
we know even in dread doom's face
to abandon time's wrinkled rooms,
coloured plates, love's marks on
bedroom walls.

Will the mild stranger's
doors be locked to our light bundles?
The vessel we board will be our coffin,
if the sailors have nailed the hold!

It was two days past Christmas
when we made this downtown visit.
We lingered long and had neither need
nor stomach left to cross the park to see
the memorial to victims of our potato
famine.

We had gotten the message.
To get out is essential. It may not be
enough.

In Bruges, six sly crooks
were charged with illegal trafficking
in humans. To date, two others
have avoided arrest. The lorry driver
claimed ignorance of the immigrants'
presence in his container though Dr.

Filip Verbrandt, sound and vibration expert, told the court that a human being would for certain have been awakened by motions of immigrants entering his container. He added that the driver's dog would doubtless have alerted him to alien presences in old Belgium where Marlow first learned of Kurtz, all Europe contributing to his making, no end of coin by trade. Mr. Domi pleaded guilty to human trafficking and involuntarily causing harm & innocent of manslaughter.

Ellis Island

Like thin battered barrels rolled to ground,
        the Irish.

Stunned families driven into fast first light
        in Sunday clothes.

Turned stomachs, stern medics, New World
        elders. Stern Inspection.

America offering, in equal measures,
        forgetfulness and food.

On panel 573, I note these names:
        Michael and Anna Wall.

Early hopefuls rushed to the pushcart streets
        of downtown New York,

Coming under the ambivalent gaze
        of Henry James.

America, we braved your disaffection
        with such raging genius

That soon you hardly knew our own faces
        from your own.

Worldwide, children cower under growth
        as jeeps roar through

Villages. Crops fail and coyotes pocket coin.
        Monday morning Wexford:

I'm home on holidays. Two Nigerian women
purchase drafts

For remittance back from Enniscorthy.
Disgraced Okonkwo,

When sent from home, tended to his mother's
soil, drank the palm

Wine of her trees. Though they merrily cross
the Abbey Square,

How strange this drab November day must seem
to bright Nigerians.

How quickly for each immigrant all can fall apart
in fits of panic and dismay.

From St. Louis, Missouri

My words are whispered from Missouri
where last night speckled children gathered
at the Sheldon Concert Hall to play music,
dance jigs, sing in the ancient language of
monks, navigators, saints, sinners, builders,
homesteaders, nuns, bakers, bankers, all
humans of a scattered crew called Irish.
Catholic, Protestant, Muslim, Jew, Atheist
too piled merrily to applaud dancers on stage.
All adults and pumped-up relatives had fought
the dismal early December night—city workers
in warm canteens drinking hot chocolate,
playing five card stud—streets and highways
uncleared, cars and semis in the ditch, a rolled
minivan upside down wedged between the
guard rail and storm drain on I-44 between
the Hampton & Kingshighway exits. Of
German, French, Swiss, Nigerian, and Irish
ancestry, these performers in hard shoes all
gathered in our bright French city to dance
one steady narrative of removal and survival.

Our Wexford People

Abdullah Ocalan held in prison they had known:
heroic tales from Turkish papers. Eight swallows
would enter Wexford coffins never having heard,
not once, of Martin Storey or Billy Byrne. Dead
in winter, they would never grace the May marina
in the full monarch light of early summer as the
harbour emerged again from the sallow shadow
cast by the mailboat train. Once, it had promised
employment, if not salvation, to our own broken
brothers and sisters looking for starts in a down-
pour outside Ward's of Piccadilly. We recall
or don't: deoir equals tear, deoraí signals exile.
For eight swallows, theirs could never be the last
door locked at bedtime, that click which bade
model county barley sleep. Where sea water meets
the spotted fields, a young Kurdish arm would never
unhook the window handle to admit the opening
fragrance of honeysuckle. Our Wexford people
would never eat our strawberries, drink our tea.

ON THE NEW MARINA IN WEXFORD

Ray Wallace met the Countess Cathleen as he strode the grooved concrete of the new marina. He followed as she beckoned him to a quay-side cafe. Who saved you, she asked, ordering coffees and croissants? Fr. Murphy & P.H. Pearse, Ray Wallace replied, remembering the Christian Brothers's old routine. The Countess Cathleen said: your new house in Rosslare is a delight & your wife's blonde highlights bring out the blue of her eyes. Scandinavian pine in your kitchen, your children's straight white teeth! Ray Wallace, you have it all.

Time was, she went on, when men would leave their warm beds to walk me across the dark fields of the republic. I'm out of business, I've closed up shop. I've gone with the Wooden Works, I told the Taoiseach, when he'd cut the ribbon & spoke his words. I'm headed for South America. If that doesn't pan out, I'll try the Middle East.

The Taoiseach, she continued, looked me in the eyes, then replied: Look at the sky blues, the lily whites of the new yachts. Observe how we have banished drab clothes, gray skies, lamentation. We are the soldiers of deep pockets & summer holidays, he added, gesturing to the dispersing throng.

A breeze from the bay wafted through the opened pink door of the café & on this wave of air Cathleen rode ghostly into weekend sunlight. Without another word. She left no trace, euro, or late, lamented Lady Lavery.

Ray Wallace walked to the Crescent & sat admiring the tanned features and bright clothes of Irishwomen parading, none sexier than she who crossed the busy road to join him. His wife didn't give a damn what people thought. Commodore Barry & the whole of Wexford could watch them kiss for all she cared. Susan Wallace was more Jayne Mansfield than Jackie Kennedy.

Before departing Ireland, Cathleen drove an old banger north to catch one final glimpse of purple heather & yellow gorse Vinegar Hill. Over Enniscorthy, she would measure what might have been against what had come to pass & observe rows of golden names illegible in stone. She knew at last her body was her only dream, that she carried the ripe republic under her great, green shawl. Ripening barley shook merrily in fields & strawberries romped in drills. Lovers lit the promenade.

BOY FINDS A SNAKE SKIN IN WILLA CATHER'S NEBRASKA

Untangled from old housing, a snake has bolted.
A boy soldered to grasses runs his finger along
a length of snake skin. What's strewn across his

field binds him to father, knots him still to home,
to solid barns, parked trucks, golden breeze. He
imagines drenched towns, gulls floating under

lighthouses. One long road. Arrived from Virginia,
she restored hill & wave to bedroom glass. What
Willa heard from her high cemetery was denial

& growing, majestic prairie. Ships rooted in
Cather's imagined ocean & Tower of the Four
Winds on a hilltop above Nebraska. Cottonwoods

rustling near the creek. The snake slips through
skin like sand dropping in an hourglass. The boy
knows this one long Sunday is no great fiction.

ATLANTIC BEACH, FL

for Richard Bizot

Atlantic Beach is one lost weekend
escape in winter time. On Wednesday,
I'd driven through snow to the airport
in St. Louis where a man in front held
a ticket for Chicago, a second for far-
north Fargo. Today, I enjoyed a break-
fast of eggs, toast, coffee in Nancy's
Diner which is across the road from
the hotel where a signed John Grisham
photo hangs on the lobby wall. With
eight hours to go before the taxi to the
airport in Jacksonville, I walk among
surfers & children & sunbathers lying
on sunbeds under umbrellas. Nights of
grouper & margaritas? Second honey-
moon love perhaps? Believe it or not,
we are of that age. Walking barefoot,
I'll turn back on reaching the pink
hotel under construction, its still,
uncompleted heights hidden in cloud.
I'm elevated in the South again; even
though some might say Florida is hardly
Southern these days, I say it's Wexford
with more sunlight & more pretty girls.
I'm the only swimmer without a wet
suit. The surfers are so busy having fun
they seem to be working: relaxation can
cause Americans great degrees of stress:
it's as if they believe Mother Superior
is always watching. Had I been born
American by the ocean in California
or Florida, I'd have become a surfer
too, stretched forever between "Good
Vibrations" & "An Ordinary Evening
in New Haven." Twenty years have

passed since I last lived by the seaside:
Courtown Harbour, Hook Head &
Ballyconniger where Speilberg filmed
Saving Private Ryan, mere mantras now
of blithe recall. As a young man I was
left behind as others gathered leaves
by the roadside, then drove away. In
this way, you might say, America saved
me. At night, in this continent's silent
core, I can often hear its old falling voice
as I drop asleep: it's the silver monotony
of childhood, moonlight through the
curtains, a mist at the level of buckthorn.
Fingers of saltwater. Fingers of sensation.
Like down, Missouri enfolds. We tabulate
our ballots fair. Fix that Goddamned
omelette quick or I'll cut your throat
is what the waitress shouted at the chef
in Nancy's Diner as I was settling
up my bill. Early Sunday on Atlantic
Beach. Swimming in winter was
unimaginable to early sixties Wexford.
JFK the first man we'd witnessed sun-
tanned in February, the Pathe news-
reels projected high onto the Astor's
giant screen one matinee. He'd stood
with Mr. Minahan on a New Ross platform
in his ancestral place, a decade before
great planes departed for Portugal &
Tenerife. Urgently, mindful of time
& bottling all, I sit to the side of busy
children in ebb tide & sun, all walking,
swimming & packing done. Once, with
my neighbour's family in a lost stone
age, we passed one Sunday afternoon
under Keating's white house above
Ballyconniger Strand. Around that level
winter's end, we were reading Sunday
papers, praying decades of the Rosary.

SUN ROOM IN OCTOBER

A girl who swung a hatchet has left
a light spot on a evergreen. Gate posts
absorb earth shade into whitewash
& white iron retreats to iron beige. It's

delayed autumn in this photo I've been
forwarded of Sligo. The lake's cover
is flat as newspaper, white as milk of
magnesia. On a shelf, potted geranium

and cactus bookend the view–as if to say–
though the room's so flooded
with light, the window ornament
might have danced, had the camera

held its ground. The stones between
pots are the simple elegant gestures
of children that say: hold a moment
longer, everyone. Admire this work.

REVELATION

Deeper moments of daylight illuminate
Bare Meadows hoar frost, a perched
Crane faces downstream the Slaney's
Unstable surface, strawberry beds alerted
By the sun's slow northward trip toward
The celestial equator. She will return as the
River returns in another form of the same
Reprise. We are bedded down in ring
Layers of time, split by rivers, united by
Bridges. We recall old spirits struggling
Still to climb our great hills, their songs
Frozen in December's air, these names
Unwritten in the big book of history. Now,
The year turns. Backing into sunlight,
We face this new day on the Market
Sq. and as we stretch to the stars we
See the sun remind us of the coming
Bright rays. Each morning we pull the
Blinds and set the kitchen table and find
Revelation written on our children's
Faces at the breakfast table and for
Them hope that all that's failed us for
Two thousand years has been tossed head-
Long into the burning lake. Now the
Millennium turns, the glass intensely full
Again of possibility like a wedding day in
The middle of July when we watch bride
And groom walk hand-in-hand under the
Sycamores. Let us dance and sing a new
Millennium home to Enniscorthy at the
Model County's centre. Let us cheer the
Dove of Good Friday peace as it circles the
Strong turrets of our floodlit castle. Let us
Turn right and left to see, in each set
Of shining eyes, hope's deep measure.

And let us cheer always in warm houses
Words of how we have made it home
Over the bridges of our old, majestic town,
Our streets garlanded in purple and gold:
Narratives of the past, New Year's resolutions.

REFUGE AT DESOTO BEND

Square-toed ladies' boots for wild Montana mining towns
are back

in style. Wines from Bordeaux, cordials from Philadelphia,
silver, china

handguns, rifles. Tea and coffee raised. Outside, under
eagles' eyes

in late-autumn trees, many-thousand geese rise in a great
wave. There's

corn on the ground, early ice by the water's edge. From
Missouri mud,

they raised the Bertrand where one guard, shifting left to
right, observes.

The wonder is how beautiful these objects remain, how
kind the

mud to wooden crates and rows of shovels. How quickly
sophistication won

the western frontier. Earlier, behind sunken poles carved
by saws,

hands, northern winds, I breathed hot breath, heard steps
taken backward

to guard the view of ancient America rising. Only to human
ways of

counting and taking charge did this gesture seem the epitome
of confusion.

from

A Tour of Your Country

(2008)

STANZAS FROM MIRKKA REKOLA

The nights are no longer warm,
The green tomatoes are cold to their cores,
The sparrows rock empty feeders with fright,
The doves linger forlornly in the low junipers,
The lights of the city thicken the November night.

My grandmother can't shake the thought that some
Thing has been forgotten–a girl's necklace or a wooden
Spoon or the cork sandal the dog rooted from under a table.
The freight train rattles its return to the mines of Wyoming tonight.

The name of the quilt is limewood gate.
Darkness drums incessantly downward beyond dogma
To tenderness softer than millions of moments of snowfall.

My grandmother says the weakest leaves from the maple fall hard,
That a deep blue dream of autumn is a hand under a pillow,
Book on a bedside table, formula from aloe and soy.

The red light from the crossroads darts now on the wall,
Now on the window.

On the wall and on the window.
On the wall. On the window.

When I can put pens and notebooks aside, I will stop time.
Solo, a grey-haired woman stands by an arbor of roses.
Grandmother. Let the day be everything is her reply.

A ROUTE TO DUNBRODY

Across a calm estuary, we glide over Cromwellian
wreckage to lowland landscape of South Wexford.

Unwearied by purpose, asking no questions today,
hoping, simply, to define King John's battlements

& the broken grandeur of layered, monastic time.
Often at evening, I had driven the Duncannon Line

to catch mackerel off the rocks at Slade, unfolded
sandwiches from foil & twisted cup from thermos

as the ancient lighthouse assumed night's heartbeat.
We traveled, then, rotated by rhythms of making

tides & the necessity of hitting The Terminal Bar
by closing time. Who were my teachers? My gurus

& protectors? I cannot forget single excitements,
swift footraces under arches, the rattle of tackle

boxes, those turnings from the soil to face seaward
the great swell channel, hearts emptied once again.

Today, Dunbrody is our final stop on the road home.
I sit on a stone wall watching waves of barley roll

in the halcyon late afternoon: the weather is fair,
a train passes, my children scamper across ruins.

Cistercians answered each urge to go by staying
put, that insistence I heard often but did not heed.

For guidance from our land, Fathers, I have borne
my children back to your song-lined paths and salted

brooks of Shelbourne. The road ahead will take us
through Shelmaliere West & Bantry to Ballaghkeen.

ALL THE WORSHIPERS

All of our ministers are busy. Their churches full
from Bompart to Lockwood. I am walking through

our leafy city, dodging worshipers' parked cars.
To walk is a form of worship as to sit and listen

is a form of walking. Your hymns emerge through
your opened oaks. The Word meets the summer air

when fathers depart with restless children, and I
remain part of the broken world which only at your

peril can you forget. My Methodists, Presbyterians,
Baptists, Catholics, Episcopalians, Jubilee Christians,

so many fill and warm your cool places two thous-
and years on, five hundred since the Reformation.

In another time, I heard old monks chant from high
benches between bogland and evergreens and taped

their song of the sun, retained the *blas* of their wine.
As all of our ministers pray hard for peace, peals of

laughter are carried from opened garages and early
backyard barbecues. To cook is a form of worship,

to laugh a hymn of exuberant annunciation. Stirring
on the air, tart aromas of Sunday coffee that will make

of every house a home, of every heathen one fierce
believer. Sing on heavenly high Sunday, all Missouri.

SPRING EVENING WITH MOCKING BIRD

A spring night hour is worth a ton of gold.
Su Shih

The gardener has centered her tomato plants
within pear-shaped towers & now will wait
till morning to remove the last of our marigolds
from front step shade to sunlight-bathed soil.

Her work is as careful as the best translator's:
each flower, vegetable & fruit earning just
the right white space & room to root & grow.
Characters become words, my mocking bird.

Drinking hot tea, we hear our old swing rock
on the whilom, western breeze. Rattle of chain,
brisk bounce to porch frame. Rhythm restored,
like a snoring man recovered—catching breath.

The gardener's hand now reaches for a spoon.
Her green dust spread about our golden gloom.

BRINGING THE PONY TO THE RIVER

Three Hiace vans and a brown horsebox
—ranged defensively—form an untidy,
Quarter moon. The boys lead a pony
To the slipway, the rising river rippled
By the grooved concrete. Now, a father
Holds absently the reins in an easy hand,
As others, to his side, observe with no
Intent lorries grinding the Wexford Rd.

With old tea-towels and a baby's sponge,
The young wash the pony steady down,
The winter light now fading on an evening
Breathless as a baby's room on a long-
Lost summer's afternoon for all the elms'
Crow beaks, watchman's warm tea
And disapproval. So still, the pony might
Be made of stone or tickled like a salmon
Into the dead ecstasy of inaction and stopt.

While town folk parade pale puppies along
The smooth white path of the promenade,
Girls and babies hoard quietly near mothers
In the vans' front seats, the pony becoming
the river of yellow light, all shapes morphed
To bright invisibility, men huddled round
A mellow beast, evening iced in winter mist.

Then towels are wrung of the river, hooves
Hupped and clopped to horsebox of human
Histories within all roaming. Unwritten. Still.

MIDSUMMER'S EVE

The fields are littered with ruins and heartache.

The towns carry the weight of disease and pain.

The great leaders will build a great road across Tara.

The small men in the small towns will fell the last oak.

BREWERY-MILLWHEEL-RIVER FOLLY

The folly drove the brewery's wooden wheel
before my years of walking home from school.

To the old people it hardly reckoned as a river
though we believed it nothing less: we had daily
coursed its banks as bands of Iroquois & Sioux.

*

Our fathers had witnessed the great wheel move:
all that we'd observed was water wading under it.

For certain, this moving wheel was another myth
to nobly sit with ancient feats performed on hurling

fields of yore & heroic nights of drinking on the town.
Then, we counted history on each medaled, hoary gown.

*

With a lolly stick I had dug
into tight crevices
around the brewery's outer wall

and bits of quartz and crooked
fieldstone,
I had finger-nailed.

*

Giants of men came to quickly roll the wheel away.
Dump trucks & JCBs came to fill the folly drained.

For how long had the wrecking ball been winding
up to strike that millwheel down?

*

Today, the old people gather on their benches still
to catch the river flowing onward for Wexford town.

Grid-locked streets, Croppy boys & blind referees
pass another hour as interminable as it is sacred time.

I leave them fastened in the month of May to regain
the standing walls I had once touched & to record

old marks I'd scraped into the brewery wall, if these
were feats I'd ever realized at all. One week ago today

in South Dakota, I had lulled a child to bed with the
promise of another Old World tale & then sat an hour
to watch her sleep on the prairie grounds of the Lakota.

OF MULTITUDE

Array of hedgehogs
Catch of fish
Clump of trees
Colony of ants
Down of hares
Flight of bees
Haul of fish
Herd of seals
Hive of bees
Husk of hares
Nest of rabbits
Nest of ants
Pod of seals
Pod of whales
Rookery of seals
School of dolphins
School of whales
Shoal of mackerel
Shoal of fish
Shoal of herring
Skulke of foxes
Swarm of bees
Take of fish
Remember me

LEWIS & CLARK 1804-2004

This morning by the lake geese and ducks
discreetly sit apart and two swans glide
smoothly eastward toward Conagra's steps.
Inside, on drawing boards and in steel
kitchens, chefs created the TV dinner.
The flat-bottomed boat children board
in summer to view a soaring fountain
is tied to its winter moorings. It's below
freezing, a wind blows and leaves scatter
humbly on these lovely walkways. Above,
cast by the bridge, a rocking gray shadow
folds old light into a shiny new envelope.
Two parallel lines of simple maples form
one young avenue of linkage to 10th Street
and white steps curve soulfully to the lake.
I am walking to a timbered overlook high
above the Missouri River in Nebraska.
Each Spring, scrubs and flood plains swell
again for water raised for its journey home.
Today, each barge captain will intone
Missouri in cadence reserved for babies.
Traffic zips back and forth across these free-
ways of pain and possibility we have inherited.
Where boats fought shallows and snags,
miners viewed lands under moonlight and
saw, veiled in mist, islands at dawn. Once,
in a whisper in 1804, Sacajawea was wash-
ing her hair. Lewis was naming this world.

LAND AND WATER

Late now:

the cut body

creaks—

scars

on the surface

of water.

As the forest

shifts

with the wind,

the boat

rocks

on the tide.

As land

lies

with no answer,

water

runs

without time.

HIGH SKIES LOW LANDS

In Norse of these lovely shores,
carn points mark
ragged angles
of our land.
Sound from sand,
timbre from rock,
roots
of polyglot borne ashore
by Flemish weavers
and bearded boatmen
of the great white North:
Irish breasted
to each newborn's mouth.

High skies,
low lands
follow Arthur Young's
and Praeger's paths through
the cropped
republic
of Co. Wexford,
our own young
steps not yet erased,
buried as deep in
slobland sand
as ancient ragworm
rising now
to note, once more,
the long-barreled gun of this retreating tide.

IN RAINWATER

They bore metal pails and bottles of Sunsilk outdoors
to bathe in barrels of rainwater filled with summer rain,
the young women. And hung beach towels on kitchen chairs.
They placed necklaces and rings on windowsills of wooden huts
cut into banks of sand, marl, buckthorn all falling eastward to the sea.

When the bravest dunked her head, her shrieks shot
shivers through the benched throng gathered to observe,
the younger children. August 15. The Feast of the Assumption.
The Royal Showband would hucklebuck the hall at sundown as first
elements of autumn took hold of sweet pea stems, roses, and fuchsia
    bells.

In turns ungraceful, the young women's heads emerged from water
and massaged with shampoo were dunked ferociously for
the final rinse. The children giggled and were calmed.
Indoors an old man scooped tobacco from a tin
and his smoke worked outward on the air.

One woman ran a toothed brush through another's jet-black hair
while a third, laughing hard, drank from a mug of Lyons tea.
The children turned. The barrel water stilled.
Striped towels strewn on sudsy grass
white horses bucking on the sea.

WORDWINGS/ARLES/CO. LAOIS

Enclosed ground of an ancient dwelling house in Ard
Lios, the whitewashed face at oxbow separating the role

of the carriage from the car. High trees, O' Moores,
garth, ring fort, Bloody Mary's plantation: there's a halo

round the moon & wide plains of heartland visible
that say you must listen for whispers still transmitting

from the glossed and runic centres of the word store.
Through brambles and barley at birth you had crawled

to don the world's awaiting tweeds as others on great plains
you had encountered had clung to rock, then trundled stones,

to address the sun from a distorted mouth in the Lakota hills.
Stopping in Arles in mid-July, you again encounter the moment

of your origin on earth: mother, light, language, love. High
above the plains, there's this leaning into blood & bones &

summer's fire though only on the breeze's hearsay can you catch
striped layers as they shift to speak. Look again! Hear the wind's

hot thrill. The monk breaks bread with the fairy, the changeling
drinks ale with the lamb, Planter and Gael swap wordwings.

HELSINKI SEQUENCE

1.

Kansallismuseo
sled-runner from Lapinlahti:
six men work to ferry children
out across the frozen land.
Under the weakly-lighted
winter sky of a northern day,
they anxiously race for deep
darkness of mid-afternoon.
In each cabin one candle glows
intimately above the Arctic Circle,
all wrapped in one blanket
of silence on top of the world.

2.

As firmly as the visitor's feet
are marked on gravel and stone,
boats mark spaces on water
and flags cuts shapes in air.

3.

Pink and yellow buildings
of the fortress, walking
Suomenlinna, women facing easels,
men locked-on to shutter speed.
The church is a lighthouse, the
light a level below the shining cross.
Light atop light I did
remember when you spoke,
the children's yellow raincoats
from an earlier time.

4.

Across your cobblestones,
under your cathedral
to a café, your voice box
cradled in the flanneled flair,
your slow descending vowels
so much sub rosa whispered fair.

5.

Hear the clank, bell, whistle
of a trolley car, rattle of parlance
from an outside place sounding in.
The Café Engel's brittle spoons
seem shaped from air, the waitress
bowed in secrecy to her customer.

6.

Where now, I ask,
the flare of light,
the light of love?
How will I know
your name?

MEMORIAL AND RIVER, BOISE

On Sunday I set out down 8th Street
            to wander
the fine-lined gyres to human rights
            where each shaved
path did undulate then wind, its wisdom
            hemmed in
brittle stone. There Gandhi, Burke—
            old Confucius
and Anne Frank—joined wise Edina,
            aged twelve
of Sarajevo, who in each cut hand had
            held death itself.
Coming from the trees, two cyclists
            whirred over
the iron bridge, and joggers seemed
            steamed like
cattle in winter fields, and the water
            to my touch
was cold as stars. Momentarily,
            this river grasped
the largest stones to halt its run to the
            luring shore
as if to doubt all fonts of kindness
            and good works.
Till like us all, Anne Frank, ratcheted
            down, it ran once more
for its attic, shuttered, ocean home
            where comfort may
not offer safety, nor dissolution rest.

BASQUE MUSEUM, BOISE

Affixed to
winter coats,
Basque shepherds,
your tickets
spelled out Boise
and beyond.

Leaving
dawn Chicago,
your train
did not waver
on the plains:
Pres. Jefferson
spun one
crooked wheel.

On a landscape
without shape,
stone boys,
you built
harrimutilaks,
affixed fish
to aspen trees:
gills pointed
to the sky.

To trust
one conductor,
cairn men,
whose language
you did not speak,
in a carriage
among strangers,
was your ticket
to the West.

LEAVING BOISE

You think the higher you ascend the Sawtooth
    of old Thoreau in Concord
standing still sublime to put America behind him.
    For you, now, these twenty years,
America indivisible from children's names called out
    across a backyard at dinner time,
indivisible from a night in deep December above
    a throbbing street when, finally,
transfigured home, you wept in joy the final hour
    of your wedding day,
finally poised, you knew, for fondness, responsibility,
    and due regard for this America
on whose sheets you stretched, the plough a steady
    sentinel atop the city lights.
When others tugged hemp hoping to pull the liner
    closer to the quay, you waved
so long when it boomed, banked, headed slowly out
    for the shuttered waters of the sea.
And you imagined a breeze that pushed at curtains
    through an open window,
and saw in early June from your kitchen chair a kestrel
    hover above dun autumn brush
on a silver Western afternoon. Today, in the rental car,
    your companions quietly prey
on alpine lakes and evergreens, the houses as we drive
    upward set into pockets of the cliffs,
their conversation bright with longing pushing forward
    above the reservoir of span
then backward into history. We stop in Idaho City,
    in 1865 the largest camp
between St. Louis and San Francisco, where with picks,
    shovels and battered pans,
placer miners scooped pebbles from the streams:
    colours, lumps, and nuggets dinging
into tin: Idaho City, then, a hard ten-hour trip by stage
    from Boise. You attend to

shuttered windows and battered signs, run a hand along
the shaved façade where
Senator Church declared for president, sounding your
friends' refrain of sawmills running
without pause, inventing a frontier city to contain—
on its muddy streets,
and in its provisional, indoor spaces—rushes of miners,
speculators, preachers, and waves
of no-good hangers-on, bankers, bakers, children
walked by mothers to shanty schools,
whole families thronged in churches for Sunday prayer.
Days when the gambler Douglas
dueled Holbrook the congressman, next day dead
from lethal lead lodged
in his abdomen, shots ringing across town till at last,
the chambers emptied,
birds resumed in lodge pole pines their mountain airs.
Inside the old courthouse—
between floorboards—gaps were precisely set to facilitate
nervous spitters of plug tobacco,
and called before a judge to account for an unpaid debt,
Mose Kempner wound the IOU
that bore his mark within the sticky wad inside his mouth
spitting downward into darkness
all frontier proof against his name. Razed by flame in May,
1867, the Irish
raised a new St. Joseph's Church by Advent's eve,
climbing wooden steps
to recite litanies and rosaries throughout the Civil War.
Last night, you drank
at the Ha' Penny Bridge in Boise to come-all-ye roars
of local balladeers
as Irish miners heard ringing in saloons rollicking songs
of home, thinking as we must,
all of us across time, of many destinies we had managed
to escape. Not one of us
willing or able to put America behind us so intent were
we to learn what we did

not know—the tenor of her ways as writ on parchment
rolls, wired faces, lumps of gold.
You wait by the parked red car at the road's fine curve
for your companions,
in green shade standing. You think of *Dharma Bums*—
those kitkats trailing Kerouac
across America, his mother heaving a heavy pack of goods
across her back,
as his father, running out of hollow breath, chased a train
continuing, always, to pick up speed.

from

Sailing Lake Mareotis

(2011)

LAKESIDE FALLING/SLIGO GLOSSES

I was astonished, too, at the impressive, clear beauty of the country and its variety, the amazing light and the sway of its healing and collusive charm.

PATRICK LEIGH FERMOR, *A Time of Gifts*

1.

Look at the lake.

Point out the lopped hemlocks.

Observe our full moon hanging in a pine's curve.

2.

June on Lough Arrow. Two swallows
forage for flies. All of our origins dot,

breast-like & tomb-like, this old land:
Carrowmore, Lobby Rock, Cromlech,

many acreages of sleep on the hillsides,
a cloudburst popping the sheds at dawn.

3.

The fox turned its back to the lake.
The wind did not bother the slipway.

We debated the merits of turquoise.
The evening was gray and the water was cold.

Rain fell from the edges of sheds. The white
rabbit pounded the perimeters of its cage.

4.

The moon illuminated the lake. The trout were in motion.

I asked for your hand and the sound of your voice.

The love of your children, the moor hen's refrain.

THE FOUND WORLD

after Robin Robertson

(1)

We walked there once, late afternoon,
listening out for ancestors, timber wolves,
the heft and stroke of evergreens high above
the road in Carrigdoon. As I recall it now,
the red scarf about your neck was loosely tied,
bandana style, your boots were as scuffed
and dry as the old leaves you pushed into
the sheltered cracks along the roadway:
we were following songlines to Lough
Arrow. I imagined or remembered
that you held my hand and I understood
that it was to you alone, among the two of us,
that the great gift had been offered: first,
among your father's elderberries, and, later,
on a walk through the great oak woods
an hour's journey from your childhood
home where you heard the great hinges
among the high oaks hollow out a fugue.
Who were we that late afternoon in Sligo:
son and mother, husband and wife, a boy
being led through night and day by a light-
skinned blue-scarfed lady? It was as if
in childhood that a book had been passed
into your hands. You opened that book,
you quickly broke its code. I, on the other
hand, had been raised among believers
to kick out blindly all spring at bluebells
and communists, to slash at tree bark
with a heavy hatchet stolen from
a neighbour's shed. I had no book. It was
not allowed. From a pulpit in the great
cathedral in my town, a clergyman,

gray and solid, paraphrased. I had been
trained to praise the heavens, hate all
that was natural to the world. The heart,
they reminded me, was a neutral zone.
As we walked, that afternoon under
Carrigdoon, you pointed out names
of what comprised this space, and these
I quickly memorized. At times, as we
walked, I clutched more firmly to your
hand. Then, as though some cherry picker
had raised me upward, I kissed the crows'
feet near your eyes. Your voice mesmerized
me. We walked on along a country road.

(2)

Save for map, crucifix and sacred heart,
our schoolroom walls stood naked.
In those forbidding rooms, we learned
of natural science that our world had
been formed by miracle that was full-
accounted in a book of truths we were
not allowed to read. As we walked
together on the paths below Carrigdoon
that afternoon, I repeated after you:
lady's bedstraw, fairy foxglove, salmon-
berry, meadow buttercup and royal fern.
As a schoolboy, I thought it a shameful
thing that my father could tell the songs
of birds and wished him silent when he
began to cite their names: first, in Irish;
then, reluctantly, in English, the language
more distant from his heart. I wanted
to say to you that had the schoolroom's
walls been decorated with scenes
from nature and schoolboys' art, I might
have accepted then the beauty of our

world and loved my father a little more.
I did not know that goat's-beard and field
forget-me-not were the wheelbarrows
on which our world depended, that history
was a patriot game written on the sands.

(3)

In Sligo, while you pulled me along
with your gentle teacher's measure,
I picked in a quiet manner among
an abundance of flowers and greens,
each placed in the left breast pocket
of my yellow North Face shirt. When
I got home, I lined my collection up
in a child's copy book, then sought
each Christian name out on the internet.

(4)

We left the road that ran parallel
to the lake and turned down a bohreen
whose ditches were all wildly overgrown,
whose stony centre shot up tufts of grass
and dried moss. We were walking
through the heart of deepest fairyland.
You liked to listen and I fell quiet too
for I thought to learn what listening was.
The sun retained its summer heat
though at times, when it clouded, a dark
hand reached across the little road. Step
by step we walked the wind rose, the wind
as quickly died way. I remember
a tractor's roar carried across the lake
like a booming cannon, clouds forming
above Carrigdoon. Walking, I learned
to fear no longer, all about us,

the darkness that shapes this world.
Absorbing, filtering, you walked to where
the road divided another time. There,
I was led inland by my returned father
and away from you. He had a list
for me, birds in Irish, and each word
I repeated after him: seabhac mara,
fuiseóg, préachán dubh, géis, gabhlán
gaoithe, caislín dearg. Good man,
he said, now I'll lead you home. The path
split again, narrowed, ended at a gate
and stile. We crossed a field, mounted
another stile, entered a stony yard. Ahead,
I saw that you were seated on a wooden
form, drinking coffee. My father said,
your children are inside. Before releasing
my hand, to send me forward, he said:
a decade ago, you looked across this lake,
then back toward land, high woodland
overhead in Carrigdoon. You found in pine
needles the spot to hide your oar. Father,
I replied, though I believe you, I have
no memory of this. Son, you must stay
here. Learn the root names of this world
you share. Test against nature's truer ring,
grunts of old that hollow ring of wisdom.
But don't conceal yourself: you must
walk laneways to join those gathered
at each noisy crossroad: hear the roar
of the accordion, the pitch of an angel's
voice. Help us recover what has been lost,
help the young teacher fresh from training
college bluetack posters to her schoolroom
wall. My father, as is now his wont, was
one moment speaking, the next quite
vanished into air. She looked up shielding
her eyes from the sun as I approached her
wooden seat. Here, she said. We're here.

THE LAST CRICKET OF THE SEASON

When I catch a cricket's high
autumnal pitch sprung from
among a row of ragged junipers,
my heart seeks out the levelest
and most insistent, homeward
foot and yard to my front door.
On Missouri's warmest days,
these many free and careless
years, I have often paused for
shade under a great oak tree
to observe pairs of doves that
quietly group under this same
line of evergreens. My children
have grown and spread, my
sweetheart is at home stirring
alone a late martini, and cars
roar to the westward freeway
bound for glory and California:
I grow invisible or gray which
is just the same difference as
they say. But this cricket's call
rocks my world—Jimi Hendrix,
Rolling Stones. Though cold
and colder this evening's air, I
can still pitch high, and I can
swing homeward, as if immortal.

A LIFE OF PAT THE SCRUFF, CHAPTER 12

Somewhere on the road from St. Louis to Kansas City, my master, or that was how he saw it, keeled over.

He hit the ground with a dull thud that rose the dust into a light cloud, the sun high in the July sky. A goner!

We were on the Katy Trail, the quite interminable path that replaced a good Missouri railway line—designed for cyclists, walkers, the young and old. For dogs, recreational walking is a definite non-starter. We prefer to ride.

The trail we walked that day was cris-crossed by shadows cast from a long line of poplars, a legacy of Governor Ashcroft, the evangelist. Once, to an admiring crowd, we had heard the great man sing at an out-of-doors Springfield soiree. My master thought him an improvement on Andy Williams, a crooner he had lately heard in Branson, an evening I spent under a porch sheltering from driving rain and violent thunder. A man's life!

My name, they say, is Pat the Scruff or Scruff the Mutt. I eyed the heap in front of me. A light twig had blown into his pants' fold, his pack had rolled harmlessly to the path side. For once he did not jabber. On a fence post a blue jay stood, but I knew better than to bother with a bird. I took to pondering my situation.

Nearby, I heard a creek's flow though in no direction could I discern the voice of dog or man. For some, the middle of Missouri can feel like the middle of nowhere. For me, as I look back, it was heaven. To the best of my knowledge, I have never left the state. My master, he was fond of telling strangers, was a direct descendent of Mark Twain. I was on the verge of something great.

He had many sayings. His favourite was one attributed to Harry Truman. It goes, "If you want a friend in Washington, get yourself a dog." My master, or ex, would repeat this to me before beating me about the nose with the *Kansas City Star*. Who is a dog's best friend?

"Love the One You're With" is an old time song he liked to holler. That day, along the Katy Trail, I took that song's message to my heart. Moving on, certain I would be befriended soon along the way. In case my old man was merely sleeping, I stepped lively. A gentle breeze blew across the Katy Trail.

Who can resist a dog in uniform! To serve the Missouri Highway Patrol had for long been the most earnest of my desires. For many years I had dreamed of riding on a cruiser's soft leather as my partner at the wheel chased, in hot pursuit, packs of dirtbags and hardened criminals. In my heart, I have always felt the siren's wail. Little did I know, that day in mid-Missouri, that those dreams were about to be realized.

THE PILGRIMS EMERGE FROM THE FOREST

Onset of evening. Exit the forest.
A band of pilgrims descending east-
Ward to the river, clambering over
Fording stones to pitch camp upward
On a rise. Later, round lighted fires,
This group from the western lands
Gathers to eat, sing, chant old
Songs and sacred psalms, and before
Laying themselves down to sleep
The pilgrims' fire is kindled high
For body heat, and to guide home-
Ward on their way those who have
Lighted out across the untamed
Lands. As they sleep, wolves emerge
From forest deep to guard the scene
While deer form a noble perimeter
To the south. Overhead, owls and
Hawks hold a watchful brief. And
Obscured farthest in woodland dark,
Bears stand guard while feigning
Sleep. In stygian pools salmon stall
As eels hug fast the lapping shore.
The river rocks on the ebbing tide.

Onset of Morning. Early awakening.
Senan walks downward to the river
Hearing from the forest a sonorous
Cacophony of song. Three hares
Observe him from a rock, two foxes
Are placed on a broken limb, and
Flocks of birds have traced a mighty
Circle in the sky. Senan knows last
Night's vision and this morning's
Show are the purest signs. He must

Bury his staff and woolen cloak. To
Found a church, build a town, lay
Some solid markers down—for it is
Time. He rouses his followers to clear
Rough ground and fell fine oak trees.
The river rocks on the gaining tide.

Towns are christened, rivers handed
Names and churches built of wood
Are burned to be replaced by stone:
The forest retreats to accommodate
The town. On the wind nowadays,
We hear still the breath of wolf, the
Breath of bear and deer, the breath of
Oak that carries home to us a whiff
Of history's odor and brightest spark,
And hawks are provided shelter still
In high steeples atop the churches
Of this town. Old streets carry tales
Told once again and then another
Time or two. From this patchwork
I can form a mother's face and
Father's hands, can't you? Vowed
To stability, community and place,
Senan sank deep sleepers in most
Cherished ground. Letters formed,
Names on parchment noted down.
The Slaney rocks on an ancient tide.

THE MONASTERY BELL

i.m. Michael J. Wall

One night in deepest winter my father
called me out to the landing
of my American home. I found him seated
on a rocking chair, his radio tuned
to NPR. Through he held a rosary, he was not
then tuned-in to prayer; rather, he ran
the wooden pieces through his fingers
playfully to keep time as Frank Sinatra
sang. Outside, a north-west wind pushed,
with a scraping noise, honeysuckle limbs
against the wood frame exterior of my house
so that, listening and quite distracted,
I was reminded of Mr. Lockwood's first
night resident in "Wuthering Heights."
My father wore a three-piece pin-striped
suit, starched white shirt, his tie shaped
elegantly into a Windsor knot so that
everything of his bearing was as neat
and as precise as I would have expected
it to be. It was the middle of the night,
late-February, Missouri, I had been sleeping,
my family out-of-town, my father was
adjusting his radio to low. Three years ago,
he said, we spoke for an hour
about the monastery that day, the ringing
bell that pulled us apart like duelers
in a forlorn western scene. We spoke
of what you remembered, I reminded him,
and all I could recall and concluded,
both of us too shy to say, that neither
word nor silence divides us: naked,
we stand together on an open plain.
I have come to you, my father said,
to teach how the Windsor knot is tied
so that all will know how you are kin to me.
Quick, put an ironed shirt on, grab your ties:
I have but little time to linger in your lovely home.

RETURNING TO THE CAPITAL

Cities, after all, are places of both eviction and sanctuary."
MARK MAZOWER, *Salonika: City of Ghosts*

Though the sun goes down, the path ahead
is clear, city lights point to many islands
of expectation—a waiting cable car,
an opened café beside a busy convenience store,
a lively downtown bar, a kiosk whose owner
smiles zestfully at all walkers crossing into
his radar field. It is a zone of hope in the tribal city:
tablecloth, bread, unfolded chairs, a waiter writing
in his order book your spoken words.
Your guest has placed her hands into a posture of denial,
screwed her face, laughed loudly as you complete
for her sentences to restore her ease. You note how
in the waiter's book of life words are stripped
of stress and umlaut, how among travelers
and cosmopolitans locals assume but walk-on
roles. For as long as you have lived, you have sensed
the limits of your wisdom though now, turning
toward sixty you note how much uncertainty
has helped you to uncover truths placed idly
under stones. It was decades ago when you loitered
by the bus shelter for the girl that did not show. Now,
yours is a bleached and softer voice while the city's
tone is tuneful to the heart, your guest's face just radiant.

YOUR RIVERS HAVE TRAINED YOU

You've got to leave home.
You don't want to do it too soon.
Or leave it too long.

Your rivers have trained you,
Oceans prepared you.
Lakes have assumed you.

One night on Lough Arrow, as the boat closed-in
On the hump-backed bridge at the end of the channel,
You piloted me firmly to shore.

You've got to leave home.

You pointed to the cairn on the hill.
The moonlight patterned waters.
A flock of sheep grazing on a sloping field.

You don't want to do it too soon.

Hudson, Missouri, Mississippi: your rivers are majestic.
The Slaney has assumed your face's fair shape.
Jesus, see my shadow. My body is becoming air.

Or leave it too long.

Wrapped in blankets, you were soothed by the sea.
We watched behind poles put in place halting the tide's progress.
When night came in, I raised you above my head as comfort
    to cold stars.

Your rivers have trained you.
Oceans prepared you.
Lakes have assumed you.

You don't want to do it too soon.
Or leave it too long.

SAILING LAKE MAREOTIS

The Saturday world glides as I look toward Seth Child Rd. I am eating breakfast at Panera Bread: plain bagel, coffee in a paper cup. Throughout the café and parking lot, this bright late-October morning, home-comers in Wildcat purple are assembling in great numbers to rehearse the K-State battle song.

In a little while, breakfast over with, boozy tailgate parties winding down, a momentous battle, greater than Agincourt, will take place: the homecoming football game is scheduled for early afternoon at Bill Snyder Family Football Stadium: Kansas State Wildcats versus the Cyclones of Iowa State.

I am in Manhattan, KS, "the Little Apple", this weekend to visit my youngest child who is a student here. Loyal to a T, I have pinned my hopes on the Kansas State football team though the inner workings of the game are a source of some confusion to me.

This is the middle of the Flint Hills, a sacred place as I have learned from *PrairyErth*, at the centre of a vast and confusing country called the United States of America. Rest assured that I am a citizen though when I say this to people they do not tend to heed me.

The hills roll gently here, there is an ease in how the local people walk, the air is crisp, the light is fixed and fine. A country person myself, I find myself among my own kind. On my way here this morning, I saw a coyote wandering the edge of a cut-corn field.

Exiting the café by the rear door, I cross the parking lot to join a group of men and women gathered in front of a row of dumpsters to which the title of *Midwest Waste* has been conferred. They are all drinking: some coffee from paper cups, others soda pop from aluminum cans.

After presenting my credentials—immigrant from Ireland—they smile, relax, resume their conversations. I join a man from Honduras: we speak of home, family, work, green cards, Homeland Security raids. When I note that there exists no such person, in my view, as the illegal alien, he does not disagree.

Three women join the group on break from work: a Filipino, a Bosnian, and an older woman from Quito, Ecuador, who is given a red milk crate to sit down on. Her husband is a roofing company supervisor, she tells me, while she herself has been making Mexican tacos these twenty-seven years in Kansas and Missouri.

Finding a second crate, I seat myself beside Maria Dolores Suarez. She explains how in ancient times, more than is the case today, Lake Mareotis separated Alexandria from Egypt, and that Alexandria, as Michael Haag has pointed out, "was *ad* and not *in* Aegyptum."

She recounts for me sundry facts concerning the history of the area that surrounds Alexandria, points out how the lake itself was degraded, drained, and then brought back to life, at least to some degree, in recent times.

Many of the terms she provides I have not heard of and, therefore, do not understand: Maks, Kingdom of the Harpoon, Tehenu and Naukratis are a few I can recall. No, I reply to her query, I have not heard of St. Menas. I fill my pipe another time.

An old sailor, settled in Quito, as far away from the sea as he could be, would sit after dinner with my father in the white courtyard at our building's core. As they smoked their cigars, the sailor often spoke of Egypt. A child, Maria Dolores recalls, I sat in the shadows listening; my job to fetch coffee when my father raised an arm.

As immigrants, Maria Dolores Suarez says to me, we pass our lifetimes sailing Lake Mareotis. On a light craft, each of us has left Alexandria for Egypt.

Lake Mareotis is vibrant, stretching far away toward distant sands. We approach the mainland without ever arriving. On our approach, the land effects the smoothest of turns away from us. We are in the United States—it is undeniable—though we are not of it.

As a wise man wrote not so long ago, no matter where we settle, we will all go gray walking along our childhood avenues. Both the Alexandria we have departed from and the Egypt we approach are visible and lighted. However, we do not ever exit Lake Mareotis, Maria Dolores Suarez concludes.

A man, bearing a television set, emerges from the rear of Wendy's. Behind him a long electric cable stretches back into his place of employment. He is greeted fondly by the gathered crowd. When he has settled it properly on top of a dumpster, the new arrival turns the television on.

A reprise of the recent El Clásico from the Bernabeu is about to commence: Real Madrid versus Barcelona. Look, Maria Dolores Suarez from Quito, Ecuador, shouts to her two lady companions, there's my man, sexy Javier Mascherano from Argentina.

We watch the game together—quietly, intently—called back onto a familiar stage, a warm curtain drawn between us and the United States.

Throwing my cup into the dumpster, I wave goodbye and take the longer route round to the front entrance of Panera Bread and, once there, hold the door for a long line of exiting wildcat fans.

To a man, woman, and child they are happy, warm, friendly, purple and appreciative of my quiet gesture. You are welcome, I say, and good luck against Iowa State today. In the café, I order two hot breakfasts-to-go for my wife and daughter who will surely have woken-up by now. Go Wildcats!

Notes

"For the Gathering." The Gathering was a 2013 Irish government initiative set up to encourage people of Irish descent to visit Ireland. It was not universally popular, particularly with emigrants.

"Opossums: Citizen's Lament." *Kill not the Moth nor Butterfly/For the Last Judgement draweth nigh.* William Blake

"Tall Blue Building/Federal Plaza/Tilted Arc." Richard Serra's "Tilted Arc" stood for a number of years outside of Federal Plaza, New York. It was removed when many protested that it was not good art. One such protestor was President Ronald Reagan, sometimes referred to as "The Great Communicator."

"The Country Doctor." In Memoriam Dr. Robert Bowe, Main St., Enniscorthy, Co. Wexford. A native of Kiltealy and a legendary figure in Co. Wexford.

"Magic Barrel Man." Bernard Malamud's first book, a collection of short stories.

"Four Stern Faces/South Dakota." Ryan White (1971-1990) was an Indiana student who developed HIV as a result of a blood transfusion and was denied entry to his school. He fought this discrimination.

"Tour de France/Enniscorthy." In 1998, a stage of the Tour de France commenced in Enniscorthy in celebration of the bicentenary of the 1798 Rebellion, inspired by the American War of Independence and the French Revolution.

"The Wexford Container Tragedy 2001." In Memoriam of the eight migrants who perished in a container on "The Dutch Navigator." Okonkwo is the hero of Chinua Achebe's novel *Things Fall Apart*, the title borrowed from Yeats. Martin Storey and Billy Byrne are legends of Co. Wexford hurling.

"Revelation." Commissioned by the Enniscorthy Millennium Committee and read aloud in the Market Square on December 31, 1999. Mr. Andy Doyle was the reader.

"Refuge at DeSoto Bend." A wildlife refuge in Iowa and home to a museum where artifacts from the Bertrand, a 19th Century riverboat that sank in the Missouri River, are displayed.

"Stanzas from Mirkka Rekola." Mirkka Rekola is a contemporary Finnish poet.

"Brewery-Millwheel-River Folly." Many of the rebels who took part in the 1798 Rebellion wore their hair short and were referred to as "Croppies."

"High Skies—Low Lands." The English language used in contemporary Co. Wexford, particularly in the South, includes many Old Norse and Old Flemish words. Arthur Young and Robert Lloyd Praeger visited and wrote about Co. Wexford.

"Basque Museum, Boise." Harrimutilaks were stone cairns built by Basque shepherds in the American West. It was common to affix Basque immigrants' train tickets to their coat lapels to remind conductors that they needed to tell these travelers where to exit their trains—at this time, few Basques spoke English and no conductors spoke Basque.

"The Found World." Inspired by Robin Robertson's "The Wood of Lost Things" from *The Wrecking Light*. Picador Poetry, 2010. To indicate how one poem took flight from another, at few phrases at the beginning of "The Found World" are borrowed from Robertson's poem. Seabhac mara (sea-hawk), Fuiseóg (skylark), Préachán dubh (rook), Géis (swan), Gabhlán gaoithe (swift), Caislán dearg (stonechat).

"The Pilgrims Emerge from the Forest." Commissioned for "Christmas Songs of Praise," an ecumenical carol service held at St. Aidan's Cathedral, Enniscorthy on December 12, 2010. This was the closing event of the 1500 anniversary celebrations of the founding of Enniscorthy, Co. Wexford. The town was founded by St. Senan in 510.

"A Life of Pat the Scruff, Chapter 12." John Ashcroft served as Governor of Missouri from 1985-1993 and U.S. Attorney General from 2001-2005. He is also a noted composer and singer of religious songs. Stephen Stills, "Love the One You're With," *Stephen Stills*, Atlantic, 1970. The Katy Trail is a bike/walking path that crosses Missouri that was created from a disused railway line.

Photograph: August Jennewein (UMSL)

Eamonn Wall is a native of Co. Wexford who has lived in the USA since 1982. In addition to his six volumes of poetry published by Salmon, Eamonn Wall has written two prose books: *Writing the Irish West: Ecologies and Traditions* (2011) and *From the Sin-é Café to the Black Hills: Notes on the New Irish* (2000). He lives in Missouri where he is employed by the University of Missouri-St. Louis as a professor of International Studies and English. Eamonn Wall serves on the board of Irish American Writers and Artists Inc., an organization founded to foster and promote the work of Irish American writers and artists. He is also a founder of Scallta Media—an initiative to promote the work of up-and-coming Co. Wexford creative artists. *Eamonn Wall: Your Rivers Have Trained You*, a documentary on his career as a writer directed by Paul O'Reilly, was released last year by Lowland Films. www.eamonnwall.net